ALSO BY EVE ARNOLD

THE UNRETOUCHED WOMAN

FLASHBACK! THE 50's

IN CHINA

IN AMERICA

MARILYN MONROE: AN APPRECIATION

PRIVATE VIEW: INSIDE BARYSHNIKOV'S
AMERICAN BALLET THEATRE

ALL IN A DAY'S WORK

EVE ARNOLD IN BRITAIN

EVE ARNOLD IN BRITAIN

SINCLAIR-STEVENSON

NATIONAL PORTRAIT GALLERY

1991

FIRST PUBLISHED IN GREAT BRITAIN BY
SINCLAIR-STEVENSON LIMITED WITH
THE NATIONAL PORTRAIT GALLERY

SINCLAIR-STEVENSON LTD
7/8 KENDRICK MEWS
LONDON SW7 3HG, ENGLAND

COPYRIGHT © 1991 BY EVE ARNOLD

FIRST PUBLISHED IN UNITED STATES OF AMERICA
IN 1991 BY ALFRED A. KNOPF

BRITISH LIBRARY CATALOGUING IN PUBLICATION DATA

A CIP CATALOGUE RECORD FOR THIS BOOK IS AVAILABLE
FROM THE BRITISH LIBRARY.

ISBN: 1 85619 084 6 (CASED)
ISBN: 1 85619 103 6 (PAPERBACK)

PRINTED AND BOUND IN UNITED STATES OF AMERICA

To my British-born
granddaughter, Sarah Jane,
and her mother, Ann,
with love

WITH GRATITUDE AND AFFECTION
TO THE MANY WHO ENRICHED MY LIFE
IN ENGLAND AND ABROAD
AND MADE THIS BOOK A REALITY

INTRODUCTION

I CAME TO BRITAIN for the first time in 1961 and felt an immediate affinity and affection for these islands that has not diminished in the almost three decades I have known their people and their landscapes. Looking back with a nostalgia that would not have seemed possible then, I search for reasons for this loving addiction and come up with the following possible answer.

Perhaps it was because I had come from an era in America of political darkness and fear, a climate in which Joseph McCarthy had terrorized the nation. There was civil disobedience used as a weapon to try to forge equal rights for blacks, and there were the various militant black groups, among them the revolutionary Black Muslims with Malcolm X at their head. They were demanding separation or death, insisting on being given the entire American Eastern Seaboard. It was a troubled time, and as a photographer I had worked in the thick of it.

Being in Britain was balm for me personally and professionally. In contrast it all seemed so quiet, so civilized, after the travail of the fifties and early sixties in the United States. I walked the streets of London remembering the years of reading about the city; literary allusions, phrases, images all flooded in. I kept putting together my own London—strangely, I had no wish to photograph it, only to store away the shiny images in the recesses of my mind to relive and enjoy at some future date.

What I did long to do was to photograph men and women and children, to try to get into visual form the feeling of tranquillity and ease that seemed to permeate the city, to get as far away as possible from the dramatic struggle experienced in the United States, to get a sense of the quotidian, to photograph the Englishness, the Welshness, the Irishness, the Scottishness of the people. I wanted to try to understand the strengths they drew on, the wellsprings of their lives—to work in the British grain; perhaps to investigate the underpinnings around which Britain's people function: marriage, family, the rulers, the politicians, the Church, music, education, the institutions which produce a nation's accumulation of tradition and ritual. To try to do a reverse de Tocqueville in pictures might work—a close look by an interested spectator with a camera.

After a short time, things began to fall into perspective. My sights began to adjust to a different scale. Everything seemed small and intimate, symbolized by the cars, which were mini (except for the occasional Rolls that emphasised the tininess of the mini). Because I come from a large country with broad vistas I have never lost my almost tactile sense of the reality that Britain is a group of small islands, and this sense has coloured what I have felt and seen here—happily, everything built to human scale! The quality of the light, the green of the parks, the countryside all beckoned. I wanted to begin work before the newness disappeared.

There are two ways to document, it seems. One is to go into a new country or a new situation and hit it like a hot wind, not stopping to think—simply to feel. This yields an immediacy and a freshness of approach. The other method is to stay a long time and record slowly and deliberately. In Britain I have done both—worked rapidly and almost intuitively at first in short bursts of energy, and then, when settled more securely into the life, more thoughtfully and more meticulously.

The work begins in 1961 and ends (coincidentally) in 1979 with the election of Mrs. Thatcher, the last cover story I did for the *Sunday Times*. The years were interspersed with work abroad. I would return to Britain from a trip to Russia, Afghanistan, the U.S.A., the United Arab Emirates, or wherever in the world my work had taken me, always feeling a happy anticipation, as though returning to a lover.

Then in 1979 my photography in Britain stopped. I became more involved in books than in magazine pieces, and went off to China and to America to photograph and write two books, and I was gone for five years. When I returned, I found the country radically changed. The almost innocent, more open society of the sixties and seventies had given way to the more commercial and greedy way of life of the eighties—as exemplified by Mrs. Thatcher's statement "There is no such thing as society." The endearing British qualities of fair play, gentleness, and concern for others seemed in eclipse.

The Great British is not intended as a definitive record; it is an eclectic view, with all the idiosyncratic vagaries of time and of personality of both subject and photographer, to say nothing of others—agents, editors, art directors, film-makers—who were involved in the various venues for which I worked. In a way, the work is a current archaeological dig. Let us cut a cross-section: depending upon where the cut crosses, we come up with images from the aged to the newborn; from the monarch and her spouse to a housewife under stress; through three prime ministers (for some reason, all of them Conservative), archbishops, farmers, actors, schoolgirls, artists, pastors, dancers, a duke, a marquess, musicians, lacrosse players—and many more.

EVE ARNOLD IN BRITAIN

1968
Her Majesty
is always
prepared for
"Queen's
weather." It
rained on her
coronation.

1968
Red-carpet
dignitaries
await the
royal train.
The Queen is
on a two-day
visit to the
northwest to
review the
results of
Operation
Springclean
in Cheshire.

1977
Margaret
Thatcher in
London
before her
election as
Prime
Minister.

1963
Dr. Donald Coggan, Archbishop of York, at York Minster. He was later to be Primate of the Church of England, Archbishop of Canterbury.

1976
A Jamaican
immigrant at
home in
Brixton,
South
London.

1977
A player with
her father at
the Schools
Lacrosse
Tournament,
London.

1977
A street party
in London to
celebrate the
Queen's
Jubilee.

(LEFT)
1977
Lord Olivier studying his lines on the sound stage of *The Clash of the Titans* at Pinewood Studios, outside London.

(RIGHT)
1966
Vanessa Redgrave in London on location of the Antonioni film *Blow-Up*.

1972
The Butler
family in a
halfway
house where
they have
waited five
years to be
re-housed.

1972
Children at
play in a
block of
Greater
London
Council flats
set up for
homeless
families.

(LEFT)
1966
Charlie
Chaplin (on
the sound
stage of *A
Countess
from Hong
Kong*)
celebrating
his seventy-
seventh
birthday.
Shepperton
Studios,
outside
London.

(RIGHT)
1966
Rex Harrison
on location at
Castle
Combe,
Wiltshire,
during the
filming of *Dr.
Dolittle.*

1978
A domino
game in a
pub in
Cornwall.

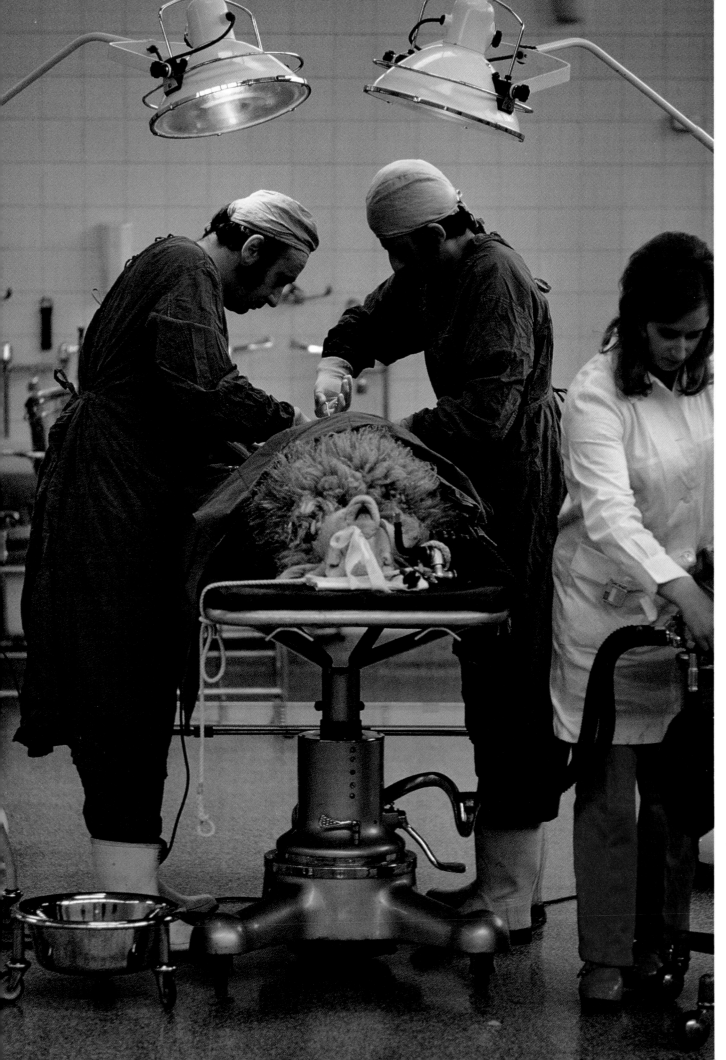

(LEFT)
1972
A hysterectomy
for a sheep at
the Royal
Veterinary
College,
London.

(RIGHT)
1963
The Reverend
A. Glendining
contemplates
a sermon at
South
Ormsby,
Lincolnshire.

(LEFT)
1977
One of the
Queen's
subjects
celebrates her
Jubilee in
Notting Hill,
West London.

(RIGHT)
1977
Football fans
in Trafalgar
Square,
London.

1978
Francis
Bacon in his
studio in
Kensington.

1972
A student
prepares for
examinations
at the Royal
Veterinary
College,
London.

1964
A hatter at Locks, St. James's,
London, blocks a bowler for a
customer. Notice the teakettle
for steaming the hat.

1978
A domino
game in a
pub in
Cornwall.

1972
Sir Compton
Mackenzie at
home in
Edinburgh a
few days
before his
ninetieth
birthday —
and his
death.

1972
Lady
Spencer-
Churchill in
London under
a portrait by
the French
artist Camille
Bombois, who
sent it to her
husband
during the
most
desperate
days of the
war.

IN BRITAIN IN THE EARLY SIXTIES there were still guineas, half-crowns, shill-ings, threepenny bits, ha'pennies, and ten-bob notes; we were still putting sixpences into electric heaters to keep warm and tearing our pockets with huge copper pennies (four for each call) to put into telephone coin boxes; and the *Times* was still proudly printing its Personal Column on the front page.

In casting about for ideas of where to start to photograph, I thought of picture stories on people advertising in the Personal Column as a likely place to begin, and *Queen,* with its new design and its team of fresh, lively editors, the appropriate magazine. Jocelyn Stevens had recently taken over the stately, moribund periodical and had gathered about him a fine staff: Mark Boxer, Beatrix Miller, Francis Wyndham, and Barney Wan.

I proposed a five-part series, one installment for each of five issues. The plan was to write to the fifty most interesting (and hopefully most photogenic) notices listed in the *Times* and pick the five best to photograph and comment on. Mark Boxer assigned the stories and we were away.

It was very different from working for *Life,* or *Look,* or *Vogue,* or any other American magazine. There, I would have had editors, researchers, and myriad assistants to check facts, pictures, and text—word for word. At *Queen,* there was a minimal staff and not even a light box, let alone a projector for colour slides, so that when one brought in colour—they were just beginning to use colour on the covers—the editors would hold the transparencies up to the light to judge them. Instead there was complete freedom for photographer and writer to bring in a story without confining pressures from the staff. There was enthusiasm and encouragement, and a wonderful sense of commitment. There was a feeling of getting down to essentials by people who were gifted amateurs in the best sense of the phrase.

The response to the letters sent to possible participants in the Personal Column story was surprisingly positive: thirty-five of the fifty answered. The thread that ran through the replies was a sort of grudging curiosity and shyness, a reluctance to being photographed, but an agreement to do so nonetheless. Television was just beginning to become a visual force in the country, and although there had been a great picture magazine, *Picture Post,* it was now defunct and its presses sadly turned over to comic books. So it was considered daring to be photographed for publication. On the other hand, photography was becoming a more respectable pursuit for practitioner and

1977
Queen
Elizabeth, the
Queen
Mother, with
Prince
Charles as
Colonel-in-
Chief of the
Welsh Guards
during the
Queen's
Jubilee, in
London.

subject alike since a member of the Royal Family had married a photographer—Princess Margaret to Tony Armstrong-Jones.

The five situations I chose were a parish priest appealing for twenty thousand pounds to put a new roof on a church built by prosperous wool merchants in the fifteenth century; a widow seeking a companion; a dog in quest of a new home; three young girls in search of a fourth to share a flat; Lord Bath advertising for tourists to come pay 2/6 to see his lions at Longleat.

For a stranger in a strange land—granted, with a knowledge of the language—the series proved to be a privileged introduction to a way of life that might otherwise have taken years to achieve. First, there was the exchange of ideas and sense of purpose provided by the magazine. Then, in addition to exposure to the five separate counties where my subjects lived, there was fairly intimate contact with the sitters, whom I not only photographed but interviewed, usually in their own homes and against their own backgrounds. Often I was offered a bed or asked to share a meal. It was instant tuition about people in varied professions, and, in class-conscious Britain, of different social origin. There was Lord Bath; a middle-aged business woman who ran a farm and gravel business, the widow Grubb; four upper-class young girls embarking on their lives in the big world, Jane Rahr, Alice White, Annabel Steele, and Susan Elliott Lockhart; a vicar, the Reverend Leslie Ward, and his community; and a Scottie dog, Merry Minx Bustle.

The first photographs I made in Britain were of Henry Frederick Thynne, the Marquess of Bath, at his ancestral home, Longleat, in Wiltshire. He had just entered the stately home business in earnest and wanted to lure as many people as possible to pay to see the de-mothed, redecorated great house, to which, as an added attraction, he had imported lions. Death duties had left him with insufficient funds to maintain his legacy.

After the commission to charabanc drivers and other charges were deducted, there were two shillings left from each visitor. The upkeep was costly: the four thousand acres (designed in 1760 by Capability Brown) needed endless work, the battle against deathwatch beetle was an enormous expense, and the lions needed constant feeding. The *Queen* story would mean up-market publicity for Longleat, so I and my camera were welcomed warmly. After Lord Bath had shown me the library and a few of his treasures, he told me some of the folklore that surrounded his family. He talked about his pampered childhood. Those were the days when the morning paper was ironed before being presented on the breakfast tray; there were forty servants on the estate; Henry's grandmother had her money washed before she would touch it. Next, he showed me his private collection of Hitleriana (this not for the day-trippers who came to see the house). It comprised everything he could garner that even remotely referred to Hitler—a vast gathering of stuff that represented an intense personal passion.

We then toured the rest of the house, and Lord Bath showed off the apartments of his eldest son and heir, Alexander Viscount Weymouth. On the walls were bold, brilliantly coloured pictures the Viscount had painted. We would all meet that evening in Crockerton, two miles away in a small millhouse, where Lord Bath lived with his second wife and their two-year-old daughter.

He had a favour to ask. He would appreciate my not mentioning why I had come to Longleat. In a shy and halting way he explained that for certain reasons he could not go into, the estate had been written over to his son (or at least that is the way I remember it), and he and his son were not always in agreement. Then, laughing, he said that he would not like to do the wrong thing and have his son cut him off without a penny. Of course, I agreed to his request, but it seemed very strange.

All through the early part of dinner we discussed the usual pleasantries: the weather (it was raining); my trip from London (the train was late); the grounds (they were beautiful); the Viscount's paintings (I was intrigued by them). Then as the butler in an impeccable white coat (and with one hand behind his back) passed among us with the duck and various vegetable dishes, the Viscount and I fell into a discussion about American writers and were well launched into Hemingway when the Marquess, who had sat through it all without a word, suddenly burst forth in anger saying we didn't know what we were talking about, that there was only one man in all the world to deserve all this talk and that was Hitler. He went on to extol Hitler's brilliance—as painter, military tactician, world leader. At this point he was shouting over his son's equally loud rebuttal. Then these two men—both over six feet tall—rose to their feet raging at each other and moving toward each other. It looked as though blows were inevitable, so I fled to my bedroom on the floor above, their shouts following me.

I was shocked—see-sawing between feeling that Lord Bath was a Nazi bastard and that he was a sad benighted creature. And I was questioning my role as a reporter—should I be helping this man promote Longleat,

1961
Henry Frederick
Thynne, Lord Bath,
at his ancestral
home, Longleat,
in Wiltshire.

or was it my job to blow the whistle on him? I feared that the whistle would be more like the high-pitched whine only dogs conditioned to the high pitch would hear. The judgement on him would be that he was a harmless eccentric.

I didn't see the son again, but next morning as he sorted out a pair of wellingtons I was to wear on a shoot, the father apologised. I told him the camera had no ears and that I would not use the incident in my story—and I didn't. But for me now the statute of limitations has run out.

From Wiltshire I travelled to Hertfordshire, to photograph Dora Grubb, the widow who had advertised for a companion. The first story was about aristocracy, wealth, primogeniture, and tradition; the next was to be "county"—farming, and a small gravel business run by a member of the landed gentry, a woman.

Dora Grubb had been a farmer's wife during the war. Then when her husband died suddenly she was left with their farm and a gravel business. The day after her husband's funeral, rumours kept coming back to her that the farm was to be sold, that someone from the outside would run it, that a special syndicate was being set up, and so on. She was broken-hearted over the sudden death of the man she loved and had married thirty-two years before, and she was still deeply saddened by the loss of her son, who had been killed at the age of eighteen in Korea seven years earlier. She knew that the thirty-three people who worked on the farm and in the business were dependent on her for their living, and she knew she must stop the idle stories and reassure the employees that she would go on.

At once she visited each of the men in turn and promised them that with their help and cooperation there would be no changes. It was misery running the farm alone and administering the business, but she did it with style. It was when she broke her leg shortly before I met her that she had advertised for a woman to act as companion and driver so that she could get about to continue her active social life—trips to London for art exhibits, dinners for her friends

1961
Dora Grubb and her friends sewing for charity in Hertfordshire.

after their shooting days in the fields, Wednesday afternoon sewing parties for charity.

In talking to her I remarked that there were two kinds of women: those who knew there was a door to be opened, and opened it—and before I could continue she took up the conversation, saying, "Yes, and then there are the others. The ones who wait for someone to push the door for them. Yes," she went on, "they are the ones who are always disappointed, because there is nothing on the other side of the door." For Dora Grubb there would always be something waiting on the other side of the door.

To continue my search for a very personal view of the British, I returned to London and the saga of the three girls in search of a fourth to share a flat. The Personal Column ad had read: "This little girl goes to America. We three stay at home. Which little girl will come and share our Knightsbridge flat? Write Box T491, the Times EC4."

For the past eighteen months these four not-so-little girls had shared a flat. They were all the same age—just twenty; had all been to public schools; the parents all lived in Kent; three were secretaries, one a receptionist. Three worked in advertising agencies, one for a film company. They earned between £9 and £12 a week and shared the cost of the flat (£16 a month each) and meals, including food for guests (about £4 a month). They brought eggs and chickens and flowers from home, and their parents helped to supplement the budget with money for clothes and extras.

They thought it "super" to be invited out to dinner because then one did not have to eat much lunch. They thought it "gorgeous" to be asked to the theatre, and "fabulous" to go to Cambridge or Oxford for a weekend. Their conversation was larded with "super," "gorgeous," "fabulous," and "bliss isn't it?" They loved living together, going out together, talking together. They found that being together sharpened their critical faculties and kept them from falling in love with someone "desperately unsuitable," because one obviously could not bring him back and introduce him to the others.

They felt grown-up and independent and didn't even mind the bath and the kitchen being crowded when they all got up at the same time or tried to get ready at the same time for a date. It was a lark for them. But now that Susan was leaving for America they would have to find a replacement who was more or less a mirror of themselves.

It had been super, gorgeous, fabulous, and bliss, and now this phase of it was over. Perhaps the new fourth would be fun, but no matter how she fitted in, the flat would never be the same as it had been for the past year and a half.

· · ·

Next stop, Gloucestershire. This time to photograph and interview a vicar, who had written in the *Times*, " 'Exquisitely beautiful Northleach Church,' writes John Betjeman, this great wool church of the Cotswolds needs £20,000 for urgent restoration. Brave parishioners achieving miracles but outside help needed."

The Reverend Leslie Ward's official title is Vicar of Northleach, with Eastington and Hampnett, Stowell and Yanworth, Cotswolds. Although all five churches required his attention, St. Peter and St. Paul of Northleach was the largest community, with a thousand souls. The others had a membership of two hundred fifty among them. Even though a church like Eastington might serve only thirty, there were still duties to be performed, services to be said, and constant visits to be made around the countryside. The Reverend Ward was also chaplain for the Church of England School and for the hospital. On Sundays he would hold seven services between 8 a.m. and 8 p.m. There were also Young Fellowship groups, youth clubs, committees, and memberships. He was Inspector of Schools in Divinity at Cheltenham—very honorary and very unpaid. He was Provincial Grand Chaplain for the Gloucestershire Freemasons, Member of the Diocesan Board of Finance, Member of the Board of Dilapidation (for vicarage house repairs and rebuilding). In odd moments there were functions, visits to the Old People's Club, the hospital, the Men's Club, and numerous whist drives.

1961
A worshipper in a church in Northleach, Gloucestershire.

Not only was his whole life devoted to the "livings," but his wife was totally absorbed in the work. In addition to the committees and church councils that met once or twice a week at the vicarage, she attended the Wednesday afternoon sewing parties, the Thursday Brownies, the Friday flower arrangements for the altar, the Young Wives and Mothers Union; entertained visiting preachers and speakers; and sang in the choir. If the vicar and his wife were lucky, they might occasionally have an evening to themselves to spend with their family.

The parish priest's pay was £750 a year. From this he paid lighting and heating for the vicarage and much of the repairs; he paid for the telephone and stationery; and he provided his own car. The hours were long, the income meagre, but he loved the work and was dedicated to it. His mission was to rebuild the beautiful Northleach Church, which had been entrusted to his care and for which he was trying valiantly to raise funds. There had been a church in Northleach from Norman times, but the greater part of the present edifice was built by wealthy wool merchants in the fifteenth century, when Northleach was the hub of the wool trade. The ravages of the centuries were many: the deathwatch beetles had got into the timbers, the lovely Medieval sculpture and brasses needed repair, the roof needed attention and was being held up by metal supports within the church as the repairs went on to save the crumbling edifice. The wind blew through the holes in the roof, and the worshippers shivered with cold. The parish priest shivered along with them and went on with his work, stopping only for the ubiquitous "cuppa."

The final episode in my Personal Column series was very slight—but to the animal-loving Brits, an important one. The ad was placed in order to find a loving home with a garden for a seven-year-old Scottie bitch. The underlying story was a poignant one: the couple she belonged to had decided to separate, with the husband being granted custody of the dog. It was difficult for man and beast. They were both lonely—she alone all day in the flat and he coming home in the evening to look after her. It had been a wrench when his wife left, but his plight came back to him even more strongly when he decided to let Merry Minx Bustle go to a home in the country as a result of the ad he placed in the *Times*. He received many letters, some facetious and silly; some concerned with the possibility of the dog falling into the hands of unscrupulous vivisectionists; some warning against her going to Americans, because Americans were unreliable and moved off, leaving their dogs behind; some forlorn letters about dogs that had been killed or put to death. There were letters from members of the Tail Waggers Club, and from people who were just wags themselves and wrote to wish her well. In the end the man decided she would go to Mrs. Stanley, a kind lady who lived in Berkshire with a family of teenage sons and daughters and horses and other dogs.

With Bustle came a list of her likes and dislikes. Food was her joy, with chocolate and cheese an overruling passion. She loved being brushed regularly, particularly her beard and armpits, and she loved woods for squirrel chasing. She wheezed loudly when happy but also wheezed when upset by a car moving too fast or by guests staying too long and interfering with her routine. In making arrangements for her transfer to her new home, the man wrote, "My wife and I were unable to have children, so I'm afraid that Bustle and her predecessor, also a Scottie, took their place. To give her away seems like selling one's child, only it is worse in that one cannot explain to her why it is necessary.

"I shall be down about 4 p.m. and will bring her equipment—her bed, towels for wet feet, drinking bowls, gin bottle for water in the car etc. etc. A very spoilt dog I fear, but one who always rises above the difficulties that face her. Had she been born with two legs instead of four, I think she might well have been President of some American women's social club."

The *Queen* articles introduced me and my work to the professionals in my field, so that when Mark Boxer moved later in 1961 to the *Sunday Times* to initiate England's first colour magazine, he took me with him under contract to be available to the magazine for six months of each year. I was to remain with them on this basis for the next decade, working mainly on my own ideas, researching and developing them as I went along, and helping to pioneer the picture-story-in-colour. I had been one of the early colourists of the fifties, but it was only with the *Sunday Times,* under Mark as editor and Michael Rand as art director, that the colour essay came into its own.

During the two years Mark Boxer headed the magazine, he created a climate of well-being and set a style that made work a joy. He was a patient, listening ear, a man who had a highly tuned visual sense and a gift for getting people around him excited about ideas. Our way of working was to talk over a project, go out and photograph, then, when halfway through, bring to Mark the transparencies or contact sheets (in the beginning, between one-third and one-half of the magazine was in black and white to accommodate the black-and-white advertisers) for inspection and discussion. Then, refreshed, we would go off to finish the assignment. When the story was done, there was usually a letter of appreciation and praise, or a cable if one was abroad.

Mark and Michael Rand complemented each other well: Mark quick, attentive, sometimes caustic; Michael thoughtful, shy, often brilliant. When they worked together, it was as though Michael completely understood what was in Mark's mind and was able to deliver it without anything being said.

They would tease me because I was a stickler for detail, and a nuisance because of my insistence on being in on the layout of my work, my feeling that it was up to the photographer to be involved at the end—the finished presentation was what people saw of the work and judged it by. When Michael Rand laid out my first cover story, it was very handsome, but on this, our first story together, I was understandably nervous. It was a picture series on Malcolm X and the Black Muslims in America, a difficult, dangerous work that had taken two years (before I left the U.S.). I had planned the overall look, and I kept niggling at Michael as he worked, while Mark stood to one side laughing. He called me a bore about the whole thing, ending up by saying that he didn't understand my obsession in the matter since the day after the story appeared people would wrap fish in it. I joined in the laughter, but countered with the observation that we were in Britain, so it would be fish and chips.

I was working in Bradford when the Black Muslim story was published. In those days, restaurants in the provinces shut at eight o'clock, and we had worked late. We were famished and wound up at the only place in town where one could get something to eat—a fish-and-chip shop. You guessed it—they wrapped the fish and chips in my story.

While Mark Boxer and Michael Rand brought in new contract photographers (Tony Armstrong-Jones, John Bulmer) and assigned top freelances (Henri Cartier-Bresson, Bruce Davidson, Marc Riboud), they were also concerned about the quality of the words. Francis Wyndham was brought in to act as idea-man—editor, sometime-writer, and catalyst. During these burgeoning years, the *Sunday Times* attracted fine young writers—Bruce Chatwin, James Fox, Richard West—as well as established ones like John Mortimer, Lesley Blanch, Mary McCarthy.

The matrix established in the early years of the *Colour Magazine* was to be maintained by subsequent editors. Godfrey Smith and his managing editor, Peter Crookston, kept the interest of staff and contributors high, and they were both still there during the magazine's tenth anniversary. By then it was highly successful, fat with advertising. The editorial matter was needed to keep the ads apart, and reporters and photographers were deployed all over the world. The magazine acted as a model for other newspapers, and colour supplements started springing up like mushrooms after rain, not only in Britain but all over Europe.

The *Colour Magazine* and the newspaper as a whole were to reach their peak under Harold Evans, who introduced "investigative journalism," for which read generic, intensive, intimate coverage. The idea was to go beyond the obvious, to dig deep, to expose the hidden or distorted facts, to nail down corruption. It was a yeasty time to be working in Britain, a time before we were bombarded with too many images, when the weekly arrival of the *Sunday Times Colour Magazine* offered a sense of occasion. Recently, a friend talked to me about that time and about now. He said he had switched to the *Independent on Sunday*, a paper whose magazine is mainly devoted to text and drawings. "It's wonderful," he went on, "not to have to wade through all those pictures before lunch."

I got caught up in this kind of investigative journalism as well when I was assigned a story on John Bloom, a self-styled entrepreneur who became a millionaire by introducing washing machines on the hire-purchase plan. Britain was still getting over the lost war years, trying to catch up with the changes technology had wrought in daily living, and the prospect of a washing machine bought on the installment plan was irresistible. The idea caught on, and there was very little competition.

Neither the respectable business community nor the bankers knew much about Mr. Bloom until the Sunday morning when my pictures appeared in the *Colour Magazine*. On the cover was Bloom with his yacht off the south of France; inside the magazine he was reading a balance sheet in bed with his wife; other photos showed the washing machines—sad, tinny things that looked as though they would fly apart with agitation as soon as the switch was pressed. He was charging 13 per cent interest per annum (39 per cent over the three-year contract of the hire-purchase), while most finance companies charged 10 per cent and large stores as low as 5 per cent. The men of the City, over their teacups, had the leisure to inspect the newcomer. It was rumoured that he was trying to start a public company, and it was further rumoured that when he was seen in full colour he was found wanting. Whether it was true that the money people closed ranks against him, concerned with what they regarded as usury, or that they thought he was an upstart I do not know—but he did suddenly disappear from the scene, and his washing machines with him. Hire-purchase is still with us in limited form, but has more or less been overtaken by the credit-card system.

At the *Sunday Times*, the editors began to explore a format that included both short pieces that might involve a single portrait, and long, cover photo-essays that could go on for as many as twenty pages, or be serialized over weeks. My first big assignment was a series on girls' public schools—four whose approach to education was different from each other, yet representative of many throughout the country.

For an American unfamiliar with the British boarding-school system, Cheltenham Ladies' College, the prototype, was like going back in time to the mid-1800s. Physically, the Victorian Gothic stone building with its turrets and its green lawns dominates the town. The college had been founded in the nineteenth century "for daughters of gentlefolk," to enable them to get an education equal to their brothers' which would prepare them for university. A century later, they were still bound by the same principles that had been laid down by the strong-minded, high-minded Dorothea Beale, the school's first great leader:

1. Religious instruction

2. High moral standards to instill a sense of responsibility in the women who would emerge later

3. Physical education

Academic standards were very high, with mathematics and the sciences at the top of the curriculum.

Here are some of the data I found among my notes: 80 teachers for 810 students; prefects ran the school; food was institutionalized (as it was in all the schools visited)—treacle tart, buns, milk, baked beans, tea, meat on Sunday; little or no heat.

Images of the students return: girls of all sizes in dark green uniforms with white shirts, silently, briskly hurrying, hugging the right side of the stone corridors. It was all earnest, serious hard work—and dates with boys were not permitted.

Other statistics that have surfaced about the four schools:

Fees—between £400 and £500 per annum

Time at which to register the child varied:
Cheltenham Ladies' College	3 years
Cranborne Chase	8 years
Heathfield	at birth
Wycombe Abbey	3 years

1961
A hockey player at Cheltenham Ladies' College in Gloucestershire.

Cranborne Chase was founded in 1946, and its students were mainly daughters of successful professional parents. The school is housed in Wardour Castle in Wiltshire; its focus was on the arts—music, sculpture, pottery, drama—and domestic science, to prepare the girls to be wives and mothers. It also taught the standard academic curriculum.

The girls had a fair amount of freedom in dress, the only restriction being one of colour—their skirts and cardigans had to be grey. Hose were all colours—reds, purples, greens, pinks, or whatever. Footwear was by personal choice, too, from winkle pickers to stiletto heels (these had to be banned later because they were wrecking the parquet floors). Hair was worn loosely, and for the most part long. There were no prefects to discipline the younger girls and to run the school as they did at Cheltenham. Cranborne Chase's was a tutorial system with the same teacher to supervise a girl through her entire stay at the school. The pupils organised their own work. There were weekly gatherings with Bryanston Boys for various activities—plays, debates, and madrigals—and the senior girls also took science classes with the boys.

About Heathfield I found in my notes only that "It has always been favoured by Royalty, high society and diplomats, and recently the children of tycoons have been swelling the ranks." And about Wycombe Abbey, that "it was founded in 1896 by Dame (then Miss) Frances Dove to give girls that discrimination of what is best in thought and art of other countries as well as their own," that 80 of the 388 girls there were scholarship students from working-class homes, and that lacrosse was keenly played.

After the story of the public schools, it seemed right to tackle something on the other side of the coin of the realm—the Salvation Army. The headline in the *Colour Magazine* read, "In this issue we explore a creation of the past which surprisingly endures: the Salvation Army, founded by General Booth to succour the human residue of Victorian capitalism." The title was "The Conscience of Us All," and Richard West introduced the article by saying: "Those who question the need for the Salvation Army in a welfare state should study the photographs taken in Manchester recently on the following pages. Legislation can clothe and feed the destitute, although often it fails even in this. Legislation cannot give hope and charity to the lonely, embittered or despairing."

It was painful to observe these derelict men—alcoholics, meths drinkers, the ill, and the unemployed—yet heartening to witness the care with which they were tended in the hostels and Eventide homes provided by the Salvation Army. Food and beds were provided, but the men in Boer War uniforms and women in bonnets felt their mission was as much to care for the soul as for the body. Of course, the numbers we saw then sleeping rough on the streets seem non-existent compared with the numbers we see now in most inner cities in Britain. In London alone now there are estimated to be at least fifty thousand homeless.

We also went to maternity homes for married and unmarried mothers; photographed prayers and hymn singing; and did the Friday night (pay night) pub crawl with the lassies to sell the *War Cry* (the Salvation Army magazine).

But perhaps the saddest sight was the meths drinkers who had to stay warm to survive. They usually bedded down for warmth in a Manchester kiln, where they would wrap themselves in newspapers. It could be a dangerous place to be at night. There were cases of men drowning in clay pits at the kiln, and recently a man had crawled into a kiln that was then bricked up, and he died.

1962
Salvation Army members play and sing in a pub in Manchester to collect money for their mission.

Memories of the newspaper-covered figures sheltering in the kilns at night would haunt me for years, and were particularly distressing when I myself was trying to keep warm in front of one-bar electric heaters: there was one particularly severe winter (was it 1962?) which the *Times* called the coldest winter in a hundred years. I was then living in a hotel, and the hotel radio, set to waken its guests at 8 a.m., blared forth the unwelcome news that water pipes (for some reason placed on the outsides of buildings) were bursting all over the land, and that the birds had never had it so bad: the long tits and the bearded tits were perishing from cold, and should food be dropped for them by helicopter? Thinking I had misheard, I called down for a newspaper. Yes, indeed, the long tits (and the bearded tits) were in trouble.

By 1963 my semi-annual contract with the *Sunday Times* began to fall into a pattern of portraits-in-action (ranging from a single photograph to a four-page study) that might take from an hour to a week to accomplish, and major photo-essays (including covers) that might take months. The other six months of the year were devoted to working for American or European magazines, either in Britain or abroad, and doing special assignments on films made in England.

The film commissions were stories on the making of a film intended as editorial matter to publicise the film when it was released. American film companies found not only seasoned actors, experienced film crews, good sound stages and production facilities in Britain, but that making films there saved money. Since I had worked in Hollywood and on location on films in the United States, there was always plenty of film work on offer.

A typical year's work (in this case 1963) taken from my log book reads like this:

1963-1 Fonteyn and Nureyev
1963-2 Chancellor of the Exchequer—Maudling. Cover Story.
1963-3 Church of England. Cover Story. *Sunday Times*
        major essay.
1963-4 World of Music. Cover Story. *Sunday Times*
        major essay.
1963-5 *Becket.* Film with Peter O'Toole and Richard Burton.
1963-6 *Pumpkin Eater.* Film with Anne Bancroft and
        Peter Finch.

Images of that year come into focus: Nureyev, the darling of the hour, handsome, wildly gifted, sexy, and provocative—and aware that he was a blood transfusion for the Royal Ballet and its major star, Margot Fonteyn. They presented to the press a dress rehearsal of *Marguerite and Armand,* a new production choreographed by Sir Frederick Ashton. The photographers came on stage and the dancers performed for the dozen or so cameras. After Nureyev had danced the first pas de deux with Margot Fonteyn, he caught my eye and indicated that I was to follow him backstage for a solo portrait. He had simply left his partner behind. As I clicked off the film, he smiled engagingly. "I am naughty," he said.

Reginald Maudling, the Chancellor of the Exchequer, was also anxious for solo pictures—to coincide with the March Budget report to the country. Since the budget would affect the economy, and thus the populace, for months running up to its presentation, the press—both print and electronic—was full of conjecture and prognostication about it, and also about Mr. Maudling, who was at that time, with Mr. Edward Heath, a contender for the mantle of Prime Minister.

I was despatched to his weekend, five-acre, small holding "overgrown cottage" to bring back pictures. The heading for the story read "The square-jawed middle-aged firmly middle-class chancellor has at this moment the power to enhance or ruin Tory hopes of election success. Some believe he could become Prime Minister; others predict a colourless failure." But it was a paragraph in Peter Wilsher's text that I found so endearingly English: "The gossip column public image is a semi-bizarre mixture of domestic virtues and slightly exotic, faintly philistine tastes and pursuits: walks small sons to school in morning, drives mini car, refuses to garden, prefers James Bond to Herodotus, detests sherry, favours dry martini, and has been known to dance barefoot on the Riviera."

To this description were added my pictures of Reggie—with his wife and daughter in their battered kitchen, which was festooned with loose wires (all of them grounded, I hoped), and with his country-squire look (wellingtons and tweeds) at the pigsty, with the pigs staring into the camera.

This cover story was followed by two more: "The World of Music," and "Our Church." My church assignment read "To live alongside hard-working parish priests and those unpaid honorary curates, the vicars' wives; the men who train the clergy and those who ordain and rule them; to go with the Archbishop of Canterbury on pilgrimage to Iona, and withdraw into the slums of Stepney."

Since I had already done a story on a parish priest and his "unpaid honorary curate, his wife," that part of the story held no surprises; but what struck me most vividly were the three black-robed clergy in the sunshine of a June day leaning against a stile and discussing ecclesiastical matters. Behind them stretched Leicestershire meadows and trees, and there stood behind the stile (curious to find out what was going on) a cow knee-deep in what we in America call Queen Anne's lace, and what the British call cow-parsley. I still remember, so many years later, my outrage when I saw the picture printed in the *Sunday Times*. The cow, the one element that made the picture, had been cropped out.

The trip to Cable Street in Stepney to visit Father Joe Williamson conjures up images, too. Father Joe was pastor to the local prostitutes, who would turn to him in times of stress or trouble with their pimps. He received me in a tiny room above his poor church and pointed out, below us, a whore and her protector in the middle of a fight. It was a terrific tableau, enhanced by a whisky bottle in the foreground, but the picture depended on including Father Joe in it (the story was, after all, about the Church). The problem was that he was inches from the camera, and the couple (seen from his point of view through a window) were about thirty feet away. It was difficult to get the three into focus. I startled the pastor by hopping up on a table (one reason I work in trousers) and shooting his head in silhouette so that the sort of half-mitre-shaped hat showed black against the sharply seen couple in an almost ritual dance of anger.

Another incident: At the same time that I was photographing the Church story, I was working on the film *Becket*. There is a scene in it in which Sir Donald Wolfit, the distinguished actor-manager, playing the part of the Bishop of London, ordains Richard Burton as Archbishop of Canterbury. As is usual on films, there was plenty of horseplay and friendly jokes to pass the time. One day I was called from the sound stage to the phone. A strong, deep voice said, "Mrs. Arnold, this is the Bishop of London." "Come on, Donald," I came back, "quit kidding." A short silence, then, "But, Mrs. Arnold, this *is* the Bishop of London." Just laughter from me. Another pause, then, "This *is* Doctor Robert Stopford, *the* Bishop of London." He was calling to make an appointment for his photo in my Church story.

Still another image persists from the time of *Becket*. Peter O'Toole played the King to Richard Burton's Becket. At the same time, he was rehearsing *Hamlet* at the National Theatre. I followed him through rehearsals and wound up the story with the opening night party at the Dorchester Hotel, with his wife, Sîan Phillips, carrying him into the celebration in her arms.

At the time that I photographed the music story, London was considered the music capital of the world. With Kathleen Halton (later Tynan), I checked out everything from the five permanent symphony orchestras to the buskers. We attended private musical soirees, and we attended the celebration of Benjamin Britten's fiftieth birthday party at the Festival Hall, where *Gloriana* was played as homage to him. During the intermission, Kathleen went off to the press bar for a drink, and I went backstage to the green room to photograph the Maestro being toasted in champagne. When I returned to my seat, Kathleen seemed to be shaking. She whispered that reporters had just told her of the assassination of John Kennedy. The news of his death had just come through, and it was to be kept from the birthday celebrant until after the concert so as not to spoil his party.

Disturbed, I picked up my camera bag and left. I went to the press bar and stood around with disconsolate reporters. The Irish barmaid offered her opinion that it must have been a black man. Furious, I said it would seem more likely to have been an enraged husband. Then I downed a drink, found a taxicab, and went home to the dirges played on the radio through the night.

My next cover story was on the Prime Minister, Sir Alec Douglas-Home, an artless and simple man. Of the three prime ministers I photographed, he was the most engaging and the most considerate. Perhaps an inheritance of sixty thousand acres of land and a recorded family history of six centuries breed that kind of person. When my car stopped outside his ancestral home in Scotland, he came out to greet me, and he carried my camera bag into the house himself. In contrast, when I photographed Edward Heath the following year, after he became Prime Minister, Mr. Heath was deeply embarrassed by the camera, and, I suspect, by the thought of a woman photographing him. When I went on tour with him, by chance to Scotland, he would forge ahead, leaving me to try to keep up with him, lugging my equipment behind me.

Sir Alec was running for re-election and was not a good speaker. His ideas were well expressed, but the voice lacked timbre, and the charm evident in a one-to-one or small-group situation evaporated when he was addressing a crowd. The morning I went to Downing Street to photograph he was at breakfast with his son. I was ushered into the dining room, where he had ordered coffee to be ready for my arrival. He explained that he thought an American would prefer coffee. I was struck again by his thoughtfulness.

When I worked out of London, the work took on a rhythm of its own, a three-stage method that I had adopted almost intuitively. It consisted of simultaneously researching one subject, shooting another, and editing a third. Sometimes the strangeness of each would make the whole endeavour seem surreal. For instance, at one time I was researching a story I had dreamed up on women who lived their lives for the most part without men: nuns, divorcées, spinsters, abandoned wives, members of the women's army, lesbians; I was editing the Alec Douglas-Home story; and I was photographing the Royal Societies.

The last was perhaps the most eccentrically British story I was to do. There are forty societies by Royal Charter, among them the Royal Society of St. George, Royal Choral, Royal Microscopical Society, Royal Society of Portrait Painters, Royal Society of Literature, Royal Society for Protection of Birds, Royal Entomological Society of London, and the Royal Society—the science society which is the most prestigious of them all. Isaac Newton was a founding member, and among its 650 fellows it numbers the country's scientific elite. It can elect only one non-scientist a year. Churchill was a member.

It was neither interesting nor feasible to photograph the entire roster of forty, so we settled on the Royal Photographic Society, the Royal Toxophilite Society (archers), the Royal Society of Portrait Painters, the Royal Society of St. George, and the Royal Society.

A few items encountered in my research: "In 1957 the Royal Society for Protection of Birds was severely reprimanded and ordered to pay 95 guineas in costs after an unsuccessful prosecution of two home county dentists, one of

whom was alleged to have sold the other some eggs of a mustached warbler." "The worst scandal in Social Royalist history came in 1889, when J. McNeill Whistler resigned as President of the Royal Society of British Artists remarking, 'the artists are departing; the British remain.'"

When I photographed the Royal Toxophilites, they were mostly older women, and there was only a single man. This Society was founded in 1781, and the group is no longer very active. It met on Saturdays only, in a Bayswater garden which is a deconsecrated graveyard, with gravestones stacked against the walls. There are houses at the point where the range stops. When asked whether they weren't afraid they might shoot into the houses, the members said that someone did once shoot straight into a baby's bath. She didn't get the baby, but the Royal Toxophilites nearly got a cease-and-desist injunction.

1964
A member of the Royal Society of Portrait Painters, London.

The "Women without Men" series, shot in 1965, was a forerunner of the women's movement. It investigated the problems of either divorced or abandoned women with children; spinsters who had made fruitful lives or not, as the case might be, without marriage; women who chose careers in a man's field but who were segregated, such as those in the women's army; lesbians who rejected men and married each other; nuns who rejected men but married Christ. The nuns and the lesbians were the most interesting, probably because they were the most purposeful women; they seemed to know what their natures required and were not to be deflected.

My research turned up two wedding celebrations, a most fortuitous find: the nuns complete with wedding dresses, veils, and a wedding cake on the day on which they took their final vows—after five years of preparation in the convent. The lesbians were to be married in traditional garb: the twenty-year-old groom in tails, and the fifty-year-old bride in white. The ceremony was performed by a woman in black clerical garb with a collar worn backwards. She said she had studied for five years so that she could officiate at a marriage. Coincidentally, this was the same amount of time the nuns had studied before becoming the Brides of Christ and being admitted to the Franciscan Missionaries of the Divine Motherhood.

The nuns said that they were in love with Christ and considered Him their husband, and that they think of Him all the time, and like any wife they try to please Him, whether it be by cleaning out a pigsty, baking a good loaf, or sewing a fine seam. They work hard bricklaying, ploughing, cobbling, and maintaining their convent. They spend long periods evening and morning (two and a half hours before breakfast) praying and meditating. This was Catholic England—the one Henry VIII had rejected, and so different from the Church of England I had previously photographed.

The most touching memory I have of my work in the convent is of the parents of the Brides as they watched their daughters take their vows. There was a finality and a poignancy to the ceremony, and one father was in tears. I couldn't bear to train my camera on his grief, but I spoke to him later. He said he found it sad that she was giving up her youth, and would be bound by her oath of chastity never to experience the pleasure of being a woman, never being a real wife and mother, but (he shrugged) she was so happy—today.

The lesbian wedding was in high contrast to the almost mystical sense of sacrament of the religious order. In my inquiry into the lesbian situation in Britain (this was 1965), the following facts were forthcoming from the Minorities Research Group: There were an estimated one million women with lesbian tendencies in the United Kingdom, of whom only six hundred were members of the MRG. (Forty per cent of these were married, and needed their husbands' written agreement to join.) They held monthly meetings in the back of a pub in Clapham, at which I was introduced to the couple who were to marry.

The day before the wedding the groom called in a panic—she was going through the normal pre-nuptial trauma. Did they belong together? Would they be compatible for the long haul? Help! what did I think? I wasn't much help except to listen, tell her to sleep on it, and let me know what she decided. Next day she called, sounding less pressured, and said, yes, the wedding was on for midnight the next night.

When "Women without Men" was being prepared for layout, the editors of the *Sunday Times* reneged on the lesbian story. The only picture that appeared in the magazine was one of two guests at the wedding, one in a chair, the other sitting on the floor fondly embracing the knees of the other. For reasons I have never understood, the eyes of the woman in the chair were blacked out to make her unrecognisable. The other woman was full face—no attempt was made to disguise her. Was this a compromise—to only half-recognise a situation? Strange thinking, but the lawyers had decided.

How times have changed, when in 1990 the BBC can run Beeban Kidron's three-part, three-hour-long television miniseries of Jeanette Winterson's *Oranges Are Not the Only Fruit*, in which there are love affairs between young girls, and teenage lesbian love scenes—and not even a peep from that guardian of our morals, Mary Whitehouse.

After the "Women without Men" series I started to go abroad more: an essay on "The Oldest Men in the World," in the Caucasus; a story on John Huston making *The Bible* in Rome; one on a twelve-year-old poet in Paris. The foreign trips gave me a deeper perspective on Britain. Within the same half-day to leave the greyness and repression of the U.S.S.R. and return to the cosmopolitan, colourful look of the United Kingdom, ranging from sari-clothed Indian women to bowler-hatted Englishmen was a visual and cultural jolt.

The stories that followed served up characteristic differences: there was Woodrow Wyatt, who saw no contradictions between his life-style—his Regent's Park Nash Tower house, his Wiltshire Queen Anne manorhouse, his Rolls, his wealth—and his being a Socialist Member of Parliament from a coal-mining constituency in Leicestershire. Mr. Wyatt may not have wanted to recognise the irony of his position, but the *Sunday Times* did. To my surprise, in addition to six pages of black-and-white pictures, they ran a full-colour page of one of the doors in his Queen Anne house. All were equipped with gilt-dipped brass doorknobs embossed with a portrait of his head. How's that for self-esteem?

There was another politician. I saw him first in France on Giovanni Agnelli's yacht, and then in London and Scotland—Edward Heath. That was when he first became head of the Tory Party. In those early days he was shy; there was about him an almost fearful embarrassment which he tried to dispel with a jovial laugh or a too-wide smile that never got beyond his jaws. I kept imagining that at night when he got home and relaxed a bit, his mouth ached with tension. But when he got used to the camera he became easier. On one trip to Scotland when the paper had organised a seat on the plane for me opposite his so that I could photograph him working on a speech, he seemed disconcerted when I greeted him. "What a surprise," he said, as though it really

1965
Woodrow Wyatt, newspaper owner and Member of Parliament for Bosworth in Leicestershire, in his garden in Regent's Park.

46

were one, when I had just spoken with him on the phone to tell him I'd be joining him. Put it down to bashfulness in front of the stewardess.

There are two incidents related to him that stay in my mind: one is his eloquence and passion about the Common Market—at that time Britain was playing the reluctant bride vis-à-vis the EEC. He was determined that Britain be not only a member, but a leading member. The other is a party Mr. Heath gave at his sumptuous chambers in Albany for three hundred constituents. The flat had large, elegantly proportioned Regency rooms that had just left the hands of the interior decorator. It was all new, and looked as though it had been prepared for the pages of *Gentlemen's Quarterly* as an example of how the eligible bachelor should live.

The Conservative Party lady voters left their male companions to their drinks and toured the flat, avid to see how their leader lived. They opened closets, bounced on beds, and, titillated, one of them stripped in his bathroom and took a shower.

The rest of 1965 paled by comparison with the politicians: a slimming story at Forest Mere, the "fat farm," at which I lost five pounds and got an amusing picture story; a BBC Woman's Hour assignment, in which their reporter interviewed a dog at the pound who barked his answers; a Sikh's immigration from India (he had had a traumatic hair and beard cutting) to work the nightshift in a textile mill in Bradford (the English girls on the dayshift said, "The Wogs leave their machines filthy"); a picture of the Duke of Norfolk with his wife and four daughters and four of their dogs on the day Lady Spencer-Churchill sent him a painting by Churchill as a gift to express her appreciation for his brilliant handling (as Earl Marshal) of Churchill's funeral. He reverently placed the Churchill painting among his celebrated Canalettos at Arundel Castle.

My trip to Russia to photograph the "Oldest Men" had received a lot of attention; it seemed as though everyone in the Kingdom wanted to live to be over a hundred years old. Later, on the tenth anniversary of the magazine, a poll of subscribers chose that story as the most memorable of the decade. Given the success of that Russian story, it was not surprising that the *Sunday Times* consented to my going with the writer George Feiffer to bring back stories and covers on the daily lives of people in the U.S.S.R. We stayed over four months and brought back thirty separate features. Through the period of the initial research, the final editing, and the captioning, I still managed to photograph four features on the British: a bridegroom, a debutante, Prince Philip, and a story on photographers, as well as stills on the following films: *The Deadly*

Affair, A Man for All Seasons, Dr. Dolittle, and *Our Mother's House.* Interwoven with the films, all made in England, were stories on the following personalities: Paul Scofield, Orson Welles, Simone Signoret, Marlon Brando, Sophia Loren, Charlie Chaplin, and a cover story on Vanessa Redgrave.

The demands of working on several stories in the same time frame makes for a heightened excitement. It is exhilarating and acts as an additional testing ground for one's ingenuity and endurance. The danger is one of overload on the inexact practice of photography, in which everything is a variable—the possibilities for error range from the film to the light to the equipment to the subject to the photographer, any of which might not be up to standard or might break down.

I emerged from the intricate weave of the various picture sessions remembering the actors in pairs, in a personal binary system that linked them through either their similarities or their differences: Simone Signoret with Vanessa Redgrave—both strong-minded, politically involved women, each gifted and individual in her own way, and a product of her national background. Simone could not have been anything other than French, and Vanessa a product of an English up-bringing and a rebel against it.

It was fascinating to be working with the two of them at the same time, and so have a basis for comparison. Simone was the subject of a story which included shooting her in the British film *The Deadly Affair,* based on a novel by John le Carré, and going home with her to capture aspects of her personal life. There was a great deal of interest in her at the moment because the press had blown up her husband's (Yves Montand) affair with Marilyn Monroe, and had hounded her about it.

When we met in London for the first time, we hit it off very well. She was forthright and embodied a depth of understanding of people that could be disconcerting, but if she gave you her friendship it was a special gift indeed, and to be cherished; she could be a tough adversary. Inevitably, we talked about Marilyn Monroe, to whom she had given her friendship and by whom she felt betrayed. She referred to her as "the Milkmaid"—by the way she spat out the epithet she was really calling her a cow. Marilyn in love had written poetry to Montand which years later Simone was still finding secreted in her (Simone's) bureau drawers.

Vanessa was the subject of a photographic profile for the *Sunday Times,* and so I followed her through rehearsals of the play *The Prime of Miss Jean Brodie,* the films *A Man for All Seasons,* in which she played Anne Boleyn, and *Blow-Up,* and with her daughters, Natasha, three, and Joely, one and a half. She was just emerging as an important actress, and this was her first cover story. When I saw her on stage at rehearsal, she was wearing the first miniskirt I had ever seen, and I was certain she had omitted to don the lower part of her apparel; but with her long legs that seemed to go on forever she looked magnificent. In the early days she was playful and amusing. There was the day she played Anne Boleyn opposite Robert Shaw's Henry VIII. It was a small scene, but they came early and rehearsed most of the day. I hung around photographing her through the various stages of preparation, from hair wash to final touch-up before going in front of the camera. I had arrived late because I had been caught up in traffic on Park Lane, where a crew was filming some Bunnies in full fig entering the first Hugh Hefner Playboy Club in Britain. Vanessa waved aside my apologies and started to talk knowledgeably about America, the Clubs, their owner, and the girls—from the point of view of what they stood for in the society we inhabited. She was funny with it, and totally convinced that the propaganda that the girls didn't sleep with the customers was utterly false. "I can just see those Bunnies," she said. "They'll be dropping their tails as though they had myxomatosis."

Paul Scofield and Orson Welles are inextricably bound in my memory bank, too—so unlike each other in personality, so well exemplified in the characters they played in *A Man for All Seasons*. Scofield as Sir Thomas More in black garb—sombre, almost saintly in his humanity, refusing to lose his kindly cool even when close-ups were being taken. Scofield would be on camera, in dialogue with Welles off camera, his voice booming out lines. It was like a battleground. Just as the scene would be at its most dramatic, Welles would suddenly fluff his words, or forget and pause. Scofield was unflappable as reshoot followed reshoot. When the process was reversed and Welles was on camera, Scofield was just highly professional; Welles remembered his lines, and there were few retakes. The crew thought it was deliberate on Welles's part; he was simply trying to unnerve Scofield, the star of the film, whereas Welles was just there for a cameo part.

Welles was flamboyant in every way. He had the biggest possible Rolls Royce, which he had demanded, and which took him, when on set, to his dressing room two city blocks away. He was dressed for his role as Cardinal Wolsey in brightest red. It was fascinating to watch this large scarlet figure lumber about the sound stage dropping ashes from his huge cigar. He was never without a smoke, except when he was performing. His rehearsal for Wolsey's death was amusing. He was dressed in a white nightgown and skullcap. He was lying on a cot, and prominent in the picture (I was shooting from a gantry forty feet in the air) were his draped red robe and two acolytes dressed in black. When the scene was being prepared, all sorts of people wandered through: the lighting cameraman checking the exposure, the hair-dresser, the costumier, the make-up person to make sure he looked sufficiently pale and deathlike. Through all of this Welles lay on his back smoking his cigar. It was only when the camera was about to roll that a third assistant scurried in and took away the cigar and waved away the fumes.

For me, Charlie Chaplin and Marlon Brando were another pair of parentheses. Chaplin was directing Sophia Loren and Brando in *A Countess from Hong Kong*, a pastiche of Hollywood movies gone by. I had been asked to do a cover for *Newsweek* and was told it would have to be a grab shot; Chaplin would not pose. I could have half a day and should be prepared to go when the director called a halt.

I was startled to find Chaplin in thick glasses; he had on a broad fedora that came down to shade his magnified eyes. In my imagination had been the supremely graceful, dancing, eye-darting figure—how could I possibly get an interesting picture of this shambling old man whom I could not stop to pose and ask to remove hat and eyeglasses?

He was a tyrant on the set, and to make things worse, he couldn't remember Brando's name. He kept calling him "Hey, you" or "Marlo." Brando revered him and was endlessly courteous and professional. But every day for ten magical minutes (I managed to hang on for three days) Chaplin would dance, and there was the little man who had captured my heart when I was a child. The scene being shot was a dance aboard ship. Chaplin danced the movements as he wanted Brando to do with Loren, and then he had an assistant chalk his footsteps for Brando to follow—a thoroughly insulting bit of business. Brando, the Chaplin worshipper, just danced along.

I had hoped to capture Chaplin when he was dancing, but no such luck. He could not be asked to remove chapeau and goggles—so I hung on, and he didn't mind my being there because the publicist had told him I was the lady who had photographed the old men in the Caucasus who lived to be over a hundred. Each day he questioned me about a different aspect of their lives. First day about their diet, second day about their exercise and sleep habits, and the third day about their work, and then with a grin—the big question—about sex; how many times? Since he was said to be living in Switzerland to be close to a doctor whose speciality was injecting serum made from the genitals of sheep into the aged to keep them young, I was not surprised.

The last day I was there was his seventy-seventh birthday. The publicists buzzed around, a vast layer cake—the Little Tramp in white sugar trimmed with blue icing adorning its top—accompanied the champagne. The birthday man took off his hat and glasses, posed happily for my camera, looked at Sophia Loren, sighed, and said, "Oh, to be seventy again."

· · ·

In the early years in Britain I was too busy working to analyse where my life was leading. Then, on a trip to New York at the end of 1967, I was asked whether I wanted to return to live in the States. The answer off the top of the head was, No, I had the best of both worlds, didn't I? I came to the U.S. as frequently as I chose; London was home, and as a launch pad for work anywhere in the world was ideal—an hour to Paris, five hours to the U.S.S.R., and varying times in between for the rest of Europe. In the plane back, thinking about living in America, I decided that the answer I had given was too simple. I realised that I did not belong anywhere, neither in America nor in Britain. My work itself made for a sense of impermanence; the change from subject to subject, from place to place, meant there was no time to settle. I tried to convince myself that I was a citizen of the world, that to be anything else was parochial, but that didn't work either. In the end I had to look at the facts. My travels made me a sojourner wherever I went. It was unsettling to face, but it was the truth.

An inventory for 1967 showed that the concentration of my work had shifted away from Britain. I had done only one film there—a B picture with Sammy Davis, Jr., and Peter Lawford (the film business was winding down in England)—and one editorial story on a therapeutic community for people in emotional distress, in which the members of the community ran their own hospital and handled their own problems. The rest of the year was spent on a three-month Vatican story; a two-month *Magus* (a film adapted from a novel by John Fowles) assignment in Majorca; and a two-month American assignment on the training of marines for Vietnam. All research, editing, and captioning I did in London, and it was always wonderful to come back there.

The year 1968 again found me at work abroad, for the most part: two films, one in Tunisia and one in Austria; two stories, one in America on the civil rights movement called "Black Is Beautiful," and the other in Puerto Rico on the pill (the American pharmaceutical companies tested it there). Between assignments I kept returning to Britain and watching the youth of the country, along with

1967
A volunteer and a nurse try to lift the spirits of a resident in a "therapeutic community."
The Borders.

the young worldwide, dissatisfied with their parents' world, search for alternatives. On a weekend visit to my son at Cambridge I ran into a full-scale demonstration with posters ranging from pictures of Rudy Dutschke, the left-wing student hero, to posters reading "Jesus not Maudling spells Freedom." There were police with impressive German shepherd dogs (to sniff out pot?). The young looked on the press as enemies and seemed particularly suspicious of me when I went over to the police to show my credentials. The police were known to be planting photographers as informers, so I was suspect. The students made disparaging remarks until one of them recognised me—there had been a photo of me along with one of my stories in the *Sunday Times* that week. Word went around that I was OK; they had been hanging pictures of mine torn from newspapers and magazines on their bulletin boards. They didn't quite know how to place me, but they accepted me and let me photograph.

I went on with the stories about traditional Britain that I had begun in 1961—one on motherhood and one on the Queen. The Queen was on a two-day tour of the northwest. She arrived in Stockport on the royal train to inspect civic improvements made under a plan called Operation Springclean. The red carpet was laid, the dignitaries were in place to greet her, the police had positioned one hundred sixty people behind barriers, and placed twenty handicapped children near the exit. She was to look at pit tips and factories, new buildings and old churches; she was to be greeted by Lords lieutenant, mayors, mayoresses, and commoners; she was to plant trees, sign books, and peer into a newly scoured garbage receptacle.

It was raining—what is known in Britain as "Queen's weather." (It rained on her coronation.) She looked very pretty in her blue, brimless hat (brimless so people could see her face) and her open-toed shoes (to keep her comfortable). She carried the usual small purse and her own umbrella as she walked to one of the two maroon Rolls-Royces—the other was for her entourage. The roads were lined with schoolchildren, old-age pensioners, and mostly women, but later there were men on their lunch break from the factories. She greeted various groups as her car stopped at designated spots—one, a hospital with pensioners in wheelchairs. Local officials took it in turn to ride with her in the car between stops to fill her in on what she was seeing.

One wonders how she must have felt about the bowlers and the bunting, the wigs and the medals, the endless being on display, but she was animated, and people cheered and smiled. For me it was a spectacle for the camera, and I photographed everything from the sweeping of the red carpet to her press secretary's checking off her itinerary, from the official who consulted his stopwatch to make sure she was punctual to her final departure on her royal plane.

I suggested the motherhood story because of the innovations then being accepted in Britain—the mother's training for natural childbirth and the father's presence and involvement before and during birth. We chose twenty-two-year-old Mary Allen and followed her and her husband from her eighth month of pregnancy through the birth of their son, Paul, and his first outing at ten days. The staff at Charing Cross Hospital were proud of their antenatal clinic and the classes in which they got both mother and father ready for parenthood. They spoke of "humanizing midwifery" and "sympathetic preparation for parenthood."

The whole thing was an almost text-book case of normality. I was called at eight o'clock on a Saturday night (I had my camera bag packed) just as I was leaving to go to dinner at a friend's house. My escort took me to the hospital, where I swished around in a long evening dress under a doctor's white coat. My contact sheets show the couple during delivery: Mary lies on the bed, her husband sits on a stool next to her. He goes into a near faint, head bent toward knees, face covered with his surgical mask. He can't bear the sight. In the next picture he peeps out from under the mask, and in the third he finally raises

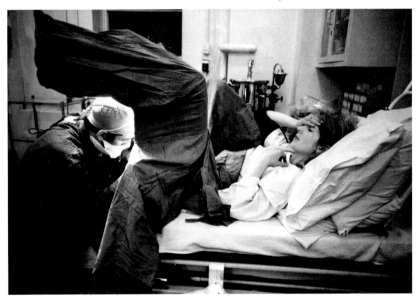

the mask to see his son. Throughout, in the same pictures, Mary is smiling, and at the end in one final, triumphant push she is laughing. The whole thing had taken exactly one hour. I could still make it to dinner. On the way there, I reflected on the joy and delight in Paul's birth. In comparison, my son (born only twenty years earlier) had been born on the Ark.

1968
Birth at Charing
Cross Hospital in
Central London.

After the Queen and motherhood, the *Sunday Times* came up with a story on the Cure in Montecatini, a spa in Italy where people go to reduce their pasta intake, lose weight, and generally increase their sense of well-being. Then I came up with a series on veiled women.

When I was working in Tunisia on a film (*Justine*), I had run into an old friend, a photographer, who took me to hear President Bourguiba address the women of his country. "Come out from behind the veil, come into the twentieth century," he exhorted them. I became fired with the idea of veiled women. It was to occupy me for three years: I was to go to Afghanistan, the United Arab Emirates (then called the Trucial States), Egypt, and to make an hour-long film for the BBC called *Behind the Veil.*

There were also two films to work on (the year was 1969), *Patton,* in Spain, and *Anne of the Thousand Days,* made in England. Britain was still pulling in historic films (this one was about Anne Boleyn), but others were only a trickle. I remember that Richard Burton was splendid as Henry VIII, but I also remember his advice to the young assistant directors who worked on the film. I had taken a very pretty young daughter of a friend, Pamela Roland, onto the set (ostensibly to assist me, but really because she was a young actress who wanted to watch a film in the making). The young men hung around Pam, vying for her attention. She paid little attention to them, had eyes only for Richard Burton, who cannily observed the whole thing, and talked to her. One morning he said, "Lads, you're doing it wrong. What you have to do is chat her up — it's chat that gets the girls every time — and poetry, recite poetry." Perhaps it worked if you were Richard Burton, with his personality and his magnificent voice. The "lads" never took his advice. They were too shy to try.

Just as the flow of films lessened I was approached by an advertising agent, Derek Harman, who wanted to represent me. There was interest at the time in using reportage photographers to do advertisements, as a change of pace from studio photography. It paid well but I was chary of doing commercial work, afraid that it would change my thinking and my approach to documentary work. With reportage, the photographer does not set up a picture; it is more an objet trouvé. One may set a situation and then let it become a happening, but with advertising one works on demand, to a more or less fixed layout, and that kind of rigidity is difficult to lose once one has been involved with it. The other danger is that advertising pays so well that it might become a bad habit — one would prefer the big money to the much lesser amount one earns in editorial work. It was a dilemma, one that still besets my colleagues and me. But times have changed, and the argument is different now.

In the seventies, photographic prints became a valuable commodity — they began to be hung on museum walls and to be gathered up by collectors. Also, my reportage photographs, under the management of Magnum Photos, the international cooperative of which I am a member, were syndicated worldwide. So one could reason that the ad, which had its one-time use, was the fast money up front, but the documentation, apart from its possible intrinsic historical value, could be worth more than the ad if properly exploited over the years.

These arguments go on with photographers ad nauseam, in tandem with the controversy "Is photography art," and the question as to whether colour is commerce and only black and white is art. It was pointless to dwell on my quandary. I decided that perhaps I should try a few advertisements and see whether they affected my thinking and thus my pictures. With the decreasing number of films being made in Britain, perhaps a few ads, if they were the right ones, would give me the additional income that would leave me free to pick my editorial work as carefully as I had heretofore.

I was choosy on ideological grounds. I turned down a South African gold campaign, a series of ads for Barclays Bank because of their South African connection, a Pirelli provocative nudie calendar, and a number of cigarette advertisements. In the end I did very few ads and what I did choose to do were ones that worked visually, and from which I could learn something about the craft. The "creative" heads and the art directors were fun to work with, and took pride in their work and fought to keep the ads at a very high level. Now Saatchi & Saatchi have changed the face of advertising in Britain. The number of agencies has declined, with agencies bought up and submerged in mergers, and now on the stock exchange; the money men control the agencies. The playful attitudes and the concern for craft have been replaced by the fear of getting the sack. With fewer agencies there are fewer jobs, so now the "creative" people are more apt to do as they are told. I still do the occasional ad to support my editorial work, my books, and if I need ready cash. I try to pick the ones that are stimulating. Over the years I have worked for the English Tourist Board and the Irish Tourist Board, finding the landscape and the people involved just as interesting as any editorial assignment. I have won two art director's awards: one for Pretty Polly (women's tights) for a beautiful woman's leg on a motorbike, and one for a campaign in which I re-created Victorian photos for Sharwoods (food products). So skilful did I become at the use of sepia toning that the client insisted I had pulled a hoax and not made new photos but was trying to pass off some genuine Victorian photos as my own newly made ones. He was only convinced when shown the authentic clothing we had picked for the child to wear in the pictures.

The subject of veiled women was one of the most absorbing in which I was ever involved. The only trouble was that, exciting though it was, because I worked alone for the most part it tended to point up my own position: isolation from the U.S. and my unwilling withdrawal from England. Although still spending approximately half my time in London, I was there almost as a visitor. As a contributor to the *Sunday Times*, I was depending on my own ideas, and seemed to have run dry in 1970 of anything to do in Britain.

I had just completed the Afghan part of the "Veiled Women" series, and

Egypt and the Trucial States were more alluring than either Britain or America. I felt cocooned in Mayfair when I returned to edit my "Veiled Women." It was a safe harbour from which I would look out at the changes that were taking place—this was at the height of the Swinging London period. It was strange to come from the souks of Kabul to the King's Road, where the young and the would-be young seemed in endless celebration. As in Kabul, there was a lot of hair, beads, and pot around; the shops took on the characteristics of the souks—colourful, attractive, and sleazy, and blaring along the street from the record shops were both Beatles records and Eastern music. Carnaby Street was more tacky and even more colourful. One felt that Carnaby Street was more down-market and the King's Road more up-market, and there were more foreigners come to enjoy Carnaby Street. It was all very commercial and about selling clothes, ornaments, records, posters, and souvenirs, but it was so much fun.

We also had flower power and we had skinheads, remnants of whom can still be seen mixed with Mohawked-dyed-hair Punks on the King's Road. Recently, my window cleaner talked about the Swinging London scene. "I was a lad of twelve. I had just started to paint a flower on my jeans and before I could finish it, it was over. Then for a coupla years I became a skinhead. Our hair was cropped short and shaved in the parting. We wore Dr. Marten's high boots—the higher the better. The boots were laced up and we wore our trousers short so you could see them boots." When I asked him about the current skinhead situation he looked blank. "After 1970, I started growin' me 'air long, smoking marijuana, then I sort of grew up. After four or five years I cut me long 'air and became a normal lad."

There are currently groups of gay skinheads who adopt the clothes and the haircut but are not political, and there are political skinheads who are said to be affiliated with the National Front, the extreme right-wingers. One of the myths that I have not been able to verify is that different coloured shoelaces worn with the clunky Dr. Marten's boots symbolize certain rites of passage. Red laces are supposed to mean that the wearer has beaten up an Asian. It is interesting that Dr. Marten's are now trendy on the high streets and are worn by the fashion-conscious young—both male and female.

In looking back I realise that I should have documented that period in England, but to me, returning from Afghanistan and the Trucial States— from the real thing—Swinging London was a contrived setup meant to sell goods, amusing if you hadn't experienced real souks; instead, I went back to America to have a look at what was happening there (and for a couple of assignments: the National Guard and Spiro Agnew). When I returned, I photographed André Previn (he was then conductor of the London Symphony Orchestra) and Mia Farrow, with their twins, for *Vogue,* and did an assignment for the *Sunday Times* on the violinist Kyung Wha Chung, who was being featured by Previn at the LSO.

The year 1971 was primarily devoted to making *Behind the Veil* for the BBC and NBC. The filming was done in Dubai, and pre- and post-production and editing in England. Working with the BBC was a pleasure. The editor, John Nash, was professional yet warm and friendly. I would try to go to the cutting rooms daily, but still try to find time to catch up with my British work. I was determined not to be further deflected from my photographic diary of the British begun in 1961. Finished with my film, and anxious to continue my British work, I chose to do a portrait of Lord Longford, who embodied so many of the virtues and contradictions of the peerage: a Protestant, he had converted to Catholicism; a peer of the realm, he had flirted with Communism and become a Socialist. He had done a great deal of prison work, and his latest venture was to start a centre called New Horizon, where young drug and alcohol addicts, and others who might be in trouble, could be helped. He was a religious man who did not impose his beliefs upon others, but the press occasionally snidely accused him of seeking publicity through his good deeds. No matter what his motivation, he was helping young people and giving them hope.

Women had been very much a central theme of my work, so returning from the cloistered world of the Muslim women, I could not help comparing our world with theirs. In the serendipitous pattern that my life occasionally fetched up, there were two assignments about two diametrically opposite working women: Queen Elizabeth, and a frantic housewife, Louise Russell.

The *Sunday Times* was publishing a series on a single day in the life of the Queen and her family. It fell to my lot to cover an investiture. The Queen officiated at eighteen such annually, and at this one there were 176 people whom she honoured by pinning medals on their chests, saying a few words to each, and shaking hands with them. The whole ceremony was conducted with the precision of a production line. The Queen stood throughout. On the dais with her were a page, who was custodian of her handbag and who would return it to her when she was finished; the comptroller of the Lord Chamberlain's office, who held a red velvet cushion; the Secretary of the Central Chancery (the department which is responsible for investitures), who positioned the medals on the red cushion; and an assistant who replaced the emptied trays with full trays of medals. Behind them on a higher level stood three Yeoman Warders (Beefeaters) in red ceremonial dress, flanked by two Gurkhas. In the vast ballroom, built for Queen Victoria, there were acres of red carpet, gilt and crystal chandeliers, and an organ in a musicians' gallery where a Guards' string band played music by Jerome Kern. Each person honoured was permitted two guests each, who sat on the little gilt chairs while the nervous recipients were being prepared by an official outside the ballroom. Flowered hats and morning suits were the order of the day.

At this time, the women's movement was just beginning in Britain; *The Feminine Mystique*, Betty Friedan's book, was causing a stir in the press. The *Sunday Times Colour Magazine* devoted an issue to women's lives in Britain — working wives, housewives, career ladies, etc. To illustrate the life of a married woman and the burdens she carried, we chose a thirty-one-year-old married to a film-maker, with two children, four and five years old, and a third on the

way. The camera followed her from her day's beginning at 7.30 in the morning to the time when she put the milk bottles out at 10.30 at night.

I had met Louise Russell a few months before, when I had used her in an advertising shoot. She had been sent by Ugly, the agency that provided "real people" (as opposed to models). She had seemed so awkward that I had suspended the session after fifteen minutes although she had been engaged for three hours. When people ask if I can recognise those who are photogenic, I say not infallibly, remembering the case of Louise. I couldn't have been more wrong. When the pictures came back from the darkroom it was evident that she came across on film wonderfully. What I had seen as awkwardness was just an idiosyncratic way of moving. There was a vulnerability, a believability, about her that was very appealing.

1971
A story on a frantic housewife, mother, model, and part-time dental assistant. London.

She suited the bill for the story perfectly. To depict her life, all I had to do was just be there to trace her day with the camera: cooking, cleaning, darning, washing, pressing, making the beds, cuddling the kids. That was her life. In addition, she modelled, and one day a week worked in a dentist's office. Life had dealt her a very different destiny from that of Elizabeth Regina.

I fell in love with Britain all over again, and was happy to be working there. So far I had done very little landscape, so it was a boon to be asked by the Tourist Board to do Northern Ireland. It was beautiful and unspoilt. The ad agency came up with a copy line which read something like "Hardly anyone has ever heard of it." This was 1971, and by the time the ads appeared in 1972 everyone in the world had heard of Northern Ireland—the troubles had started.

We thought it might give us a fresh look to do aerial views, and so arrangements were made for me to fly in Air Force planes to get the photos. When the officials found that I was a woman, they refused to let me do it; they said that regulations prohibited their piloting a woman. I asked if this were a leftover from the superstition about women in ships bringing bad luck, but they just grinned sheepishly and mumbled that they couldn't go against regulations. We had to rent a commercial craft, and were unable to find a helicopter, so had to settle for a single-engine plane with the door removed, me strapped in and shooting out of the open doorframe.

It is best to shoot from the air after rainfall because rain washes the atmosphere and makes for greater clarity of picture. Unfortunately, we ran into sudden gusts of high wind. I'm glad that the pilot didn't tell me until afterwards that we had hit a Force Eight gale and he was afraid that when we landed the light airplane might turn over. Those were my first and last aerial shots. After that, all photography was on terra firma.

One other thing I recall about the Northern Ireland take—the pubs. At one point there were two public houses directly opposite each other. One had a crusty old feeling that would have American tourists drooling over it, but in which the people imbibing did not look very interesting, and the other, in which the people looked great, was pedestrian-looking. When I suggested moving the better-lookers across the street to the better-looking pub, the tourist-board man seemed to shiver. I was shushed, taken outside, and asked if I wanted to start a civil war. One was a Catholic venue, the other a Protestant—and never the twain shall meet.

Except for a trip to Germany to document the 1972 Olympics in pictures and words for *Nouveau Fotocinema*, my work that year was chiefly in Britain. It began with a trip to Newcastle, to report on men at work in the shipyards. This was part of a series the *Sunday Times* was preparing on manhood. The idea was that men's identity is strongly bound to their work, and that the shipyard would give us a unified story with the ship as the bond. There were a great variety of workers involved: draughtsmen, joiners, plumbers, electricians, welders, painters, shipwrights, boilermakers, marine engineers, supervisors. Those were the days when Britain still had a ship-building industry. The men were finishing up a 250,000-ton super-tanker at the Swan Hunter shipyard on Tyneside.

One of the men commented to Peter Crookston that "the manual workers in the yard had the same tough, confident aura about them as miners do, partly because of the dangerous physical nature of their work, but also because they are masters of their own activities with a freedom that is just not possible in other industries. There's nobody standing over them while they work." One was struck by their fierce individuality and their ability to express themselves verbally. For the most part, they were local people who did what they did because their fathers and grandfathers had worked with their hands at the same jobs. When asked whether they were happy in their jobs, the men looked puzzled: they take life as it comes. Any ambitions? Yes, they would like to win the pools, to get a new car or a stereo without having to save up for them. Visually, it was amusing to see the working men in hard-hats, the executives in bowlers, and to witness yet another class distinction: the executives had cream with their tea, the men milk.

It felt good to be working in Britain, so I settled in for the rest of the year, snug in my Mayfair eyrie, going out to photograph and returning home to look out over what was then a neighbourhood: an Italian restaurant, Trattoria Fiore; an Italian grocery cum greengrocery, Ambrose; a fishmonger, MacFisheries; a dairy; an ironmonger; and for a brief blessed period, a Bumpus bookshop. Farther down the road there was the chemist, and two of the most elegant meat shops anywhere in the Western world: Bailey's the poulterer, and Allen Butcher (that's the way they answered the telephone). Allen's has been in Mayfair for over 250 years, but at its current premises for only 125 years.

With a long lens I would survey the displays in the shop windows, then I would phone down and place an order for the specific fish or whatever that I wanted to eat that day, the book I wanted to read, the groceries, milk, cheese, vegetables, fruit, etc., that were needed, and all would be delivered. It was an amusing way to shop. But most of that is gone now (of course Allen Butcher is still there), replaced by bath shops in questionable taste, men's bespoke tailoring shops, and antique shops catering to the Arab and American tourist trade.

· · ·

Ever since the story on the Scottie Merry Minx Bustle, I had wanted to understand more about the British in their relationship to their animals, so the Royal Veterinary College, with its teaching about domestic animals, was a welcome assignment. It was strange to see a live horse trundled into a green-painted amphitheatre where students were seated busily taking notes. Apparently, the same animals were used again and again for demonstration: there was one mongrel bitch who was used to show the proper procedure for taking temperature anally and who always tried to escape before the students (there was always one to use the thermometer and one to hold the dog) could get started.

Unlike doctors who practise on humans and thus study only a single anatomy, the veterinary practitioner has to study seven domestic anatomies—cat, dog, horse, sheep, pig, cow, and chicken—before graduating the five-year course. Students could be spotted through the various halls studying different skeletons in a surreal juxtaposition of Victorian hall, old bones, and live animals. We saw everything from the animal clinic to which small, anxious boys brought suffering pets, to the operating theatre in which a famous racehorse was being operated for a brain tumour, to the hysterectomy of a sheep, its mouth neatly tied in a natty double surgical-gauze bow during anaesthesia.

After this, there was a story on stress in the persons of Mrs. Butler and her family. My instructions were to focus on the stress, not the unsightly surroundings, the poverty, the sense of futility and failure, and the tranquillizers that made existence bearable. It was, of course, not possible to ignore the facts that the Butlers had lost their home, the husband was unemployed, and that the five of them (there were three children) had been waiting in close-packed squalour for almost five years for the Council to re-house them. It was a telling story, but how to tell it?

When Michael Rand had called to discuss the pictures, I said that obviously it was a black-and-white story, expecting him to disagree and to twit me about taking the easy way out, but he didn't, despite the fact that practically everything printed in the

1972
Mrs. Butler in a
halfway house.
London.

magazine had by the early seventies gone over to colour. It was, after all, called the *Colour Magazine.*

I could not have been more wrong. The black and white, with its intermediate tones of grey, managed to look deeply depressing without showing any of the pathos and pain etched on the map of Mrs. Butler's thirty-eight-year-old face. It showed her as an abstraction, removed from our involvement, our empathy. What to do? I returned to colour, shooting for form (not colour) and muting the colour by simply using the available light so that the result was a rich monochrome.

Mrs. Butler became a woman under stress on whose countenance was lined her daily struggle for survival. We ran the portrait full page, and this, along with Pauline Peters' eloquent text, made it possible to see her as a woman of spirit. The day after the story ran, the *Sunday Times* started receiving money for the family (one of the editors estimated three thousand pounds); the husband was offered a job; and the family was re-housed.

I kept wondering how the Butlers felt about seeing themselves in print. Had I invaded their privacy too blatantly and shamed them, in spite of trying to help them? I tussled with the reporter's dilemma of how best to do one's job without hurting the people one wants to help. I believe that one function of the photographer is to show the viewer something he would not have seen if the photographer hadn't shown it to him, so tangible evidence that people had seen—and responded to—the message from one of my pictures was gratifying. It happened to me only the once, but those were generous times. Nowadays, with the increased numbers of people living rough on the streets, and with the multitude of problems facing so many, it is less likely to happen. It is easier to identify with single people than with a mass; one tends to tune out on numbers. Also, I question whether the welter of images that bombard us daily, both print and electronic—what a friend calls "social wallpaper"—gets lost in our overloaded brain circuits, and de-sensitizes our emotions. There is almost too much to absorb.

The help received by the Butlers was a heady bonus, and one that encouraged me to do more portraiture—what Alexey Brodovitch, my photographic mentor, called "portrait in action," a phrase that meant the opposite from the stationary mug shot. The images can consist of a single photo, if one is fortunate enough to be able to tell the story in one definitive image, as I believe I was with Lady Spencer-Churchill, Winston's widow, or in a series of pictures to show different facets of the personality, as happened with Sir Compton Mackenzie.

At the *Sunday Times'* suggestion, I called Lady Spencer-Churchill to request a sitting, and she accepted graciously, naming a Tuesday afternoon. That was the day her hairdresser would have come and she would feel at her best. She was in her mid-eighties, tall, straight, and still beautiful, but camera shy. She had preferred her life to be lived as background to her husband's.

She suggested that I might want to photograph her the way Toni Frissell, another American photographer, had—behind a Louis XVI escritoire. This had been for *Vogue*, during the war. It was something she obviously wanted, so she sat and smiled as I clicked away. Then we went on a tour of her Prince's Gate flat to find other locations. There was a perfect one: in front of an oil painting of a bulldog by Camille Bombois, a French painter who had sent the painting to Churchill during the Blitz. Churchill had loved it. A secretary adjusted a chair, and the lady lowered herself into it below the scowling beast. The whole thing took exactly fourteen minutes. When I was leaving, she asked if she could see the pictures before publication, not to edit them, but out of curiosity. It isn't a good idea to show people pictures before publication. What if the subject hates the pictures? What is the responsibility of the photographer—publish? reshoot? withdraw the picture? But the "Lady and the Bulldog" (as the *Sunday Times* dubbed it) was respectable—so why not show? We agreed that I would call in with the pictures in three days' time when they were processed. When I arrived, complete with projector and slides, and we had managed to darken her study, she looked at herself magnified on the wall and said that she had always liked that picture of Pompidou's; I was a little thrown by her confusion and asked if I might see the painting again, just so that I could write a correct caption about it. She, her secretary, and I trooped into the room where the painting hung and looked at the painting. I made some notes. Lady Spencer-Churchill looked at the bold signature, Camille Bombois, and said, Yes, she was happy to be photographed with a painting by Pompidou. The secretary gave me the eye: it was time to leave. Lady Spencer-Churchill smiled, took me to the door, and shook hands.

Sir Compton Mackenzie, the writer, couldn't have been more different. Godfrey Smith, who wrote the article, called it the "Unclouded Memory." A few days before Sir Compton's ninetieth birthday I flew up to Edinburgh with an assistant to photograph him. Normally I prefer to work alone, especially for portraits—the presence of an extra person seems to change the situation, to make it more difficult to establish contact, the most important ingredient in photographing people. But in this case I had asked Chris Mead to come with me. The idea was to be able to work quickly and seamlessly, with Chris loading film and doing all the necessary small jobs to leave me free to give full attention to the ancient.

Something strange happened when we walked into the Mackenzie drawing-room. The four of us—Sir Compton Mackenzie, Lady Mackenzie, Chris Mead, and I—fell in love. There is no other way to describe it. It must parallel what a religious must mean when he speaks of being in a state of grace, or what a drug addict tries to achieve on a high. It was—literally was—bliss.

I remember shooting very little, listening hard. Mackenzie talked—he remembered his nanny, his first love, from the time he was two years old, and described her with a writer's minute graphic detail. He spoke about his autobiography (he hoped to write a coda); about the 112 books he thought he had written; about the women in his (love) life—no woman had ever refused him; about the fact that he had 20 more novels in him, one of them to be called *The Cabinet of Women*, about the first woman Prime Minister. This was prescient of him; this was 1972, and Mrs. Thatcher still seven years away. What would he have made of her?

He rested while we went to lunch. When we returned, he was in a four-poster bed, and the sense of euphoria experienced in the morning still held. There was one more roll of film to do of him in bed. Then he kissed me good-bye and talked about his happiness that day. I understood why women couldn't resist him. I wished him a wonderful birthday and tiptoed from the room. Three days later the BBC came to do a celebratory programme for his nine-tieth birthday. After the director and crew left, he quietly died—a happy man.

The year's stay in England had been tranquil and fulfilling. I had also learned a lot about portraiture, but it was time to move on, time for something more challenging, time to stretch myself on something more daring, more difficult; to go away. The answer was a difficult story, "Black in South Africa."

I returned from South Africa heartsick, suffering from heartache to an extent that left my doctor concerned that I might have suffered a mild heart attack. X-rays and thumpings revealed nothing. It was a physical manifestation of emotional distress suffered at what I had witnessed. I went back to staying home, enjoying London, and peering at the shops through my long lens. There were friends, theatre, art exhibitions, and visits to Ireland to spend weekends and holidays with John Huston. Gradually, the images of poverty and degradation of South Africa receded, the pain disappeared from my heart, and I began to look forward to working abroad again.

From the South African story, in 1973, to the beginning of 1975, when I returned to London for a long stretch to begin work on my first book, my stays in London were brief, spent mainly editing and captioning work brought in from abroad, and researching further work to be done elsewhere. In 1973 and 1974 I did two stories in France—one on the Picasso heirs and one on Malraux (with Bruce Chatwin)—and a story on Galya, a Russian model, in Italy. The highlights for 1975 were the film *The Man Who Would Be King*, in Morocco, and a story in the U.S.S.R. called "The Golden Road to Samarkand."

The years 1975 and 1976 were devoted to editing and writing two books for Knopf: *The Unretouched Woman*, about women I had photographed (in colour and black and white) around the world, and *Flashback! The 50's*, a more or less political picture book on America in the fifties, the period from Joseph McCarthy to Malcolm X. I had known and photographed them both. The years with the books were stimulating but fragmented, spent between America, where my editor-cum-publisher, Robert Gottlieb, was, and London, where my pictures and my base were.

There was so much to learn about writing books—as opposed to writing for magazines and newspapers; so much to learn about layout; so much to learn about production. It was a burgeoning, a birth, a freshness, and again that fine feeling of belonging I hadn't experienced in years—might it really be that I was having the best of both worlds?

The Unretouched Woman was published in 1976, so there were frequent trips to America for publication and promotion, and trips back to London because the BBC was making a half-hour film on me called *The Unretouched Woman*. Then back to America for the two-hundredth anniversary of the country, and a small stint at the Democratic National Convention for the nomination of Jimmy Carter.

The year 1977 was lively. Besides working on the publication of *Flashback! The 50's*, there was the birth in Glasgow of my grandson, Michael. It was wonderful to be a grandmother, and in order to spend as much time as possible in England to watch him grow I took on assignments here. There was a story on Brent Cross, Britain's first super supermarket; a story on women's sport; a series on the Queen's Jubilee, with sidelights on the anti-Jubilee (a tongue-in-cheek celebration by anti-Royalists, which although not very large was handled with typical British good humour and irony).

Then off to Paris to do a special reportage for French *Vogue*. Every spring and autumn the magazine chooses a guest editor who is given fifty pages and the freedom to cover any topic that is of interest to him. On this occasion they selected Joe Losey, the film director, he chose me, and together we decided to document the hoopla backstage at the Fashion Collections. In between times I was working on a photographic profile of Margaret Thatcher.

The *Sunday Times* wanted me to do two cover essays. The working title was "Two Women in Pursuit of Power." One was Mrs. Gandhi, who was out of power after the Emergency, and was trying to get back, and the other was Mrs. Thatcher, who was trying to get in. The Thatcher story started with my going to the Orkneys, to Blackpool for the Conservative Party Conference, and to a

Putney day-care centre for the aged, among other places. The story was begun in 1977 and continued through 1978.

It had been an advantage to be a woman photographing the other Prime Ministers, Sir Alec Douglas-Home and Edward Heath. Men like being photographed by a woman—there is often an undercurrent of teasing, of flirtatiousness. The men would show off their masculinity and play the hero in a way they might have found embarrassing if the photographer had been another man.

Women, too, like to have a woman at the other end of the camera. There is generally a bond between the women and a curiosity, each for the other, that adds a piquant flavour to the session and is reflected in the pictures. At least this had been my experience until I picked up the camera to photograph Mrs. Thatcher. She was a law unto herself; anything that touched her, at least in those days, had to be firmly in her control.

That year, during which I must have seen her on at least fifteen separate days, it was virtually impossible to establish contact. She was readily available to the camera, affable enough, she smiled good morning and goodnight, but she called the shots, and inevitably there was a rigidity in the pictures.

We first met, and aptly it seemed, in a grocery shop in the Orkneys, where she made the rounds, commenting on the prices. She bought an Orkney cheese. (She bought food to take home wherever she went—was this a reversal

of her girlhood? Had she perhaps wanted to be the customer, not the grocer's daughter—although she seemed proud of her origins and used them skilfully in her campaign?) She picked up the cheese, signalled for me to photograph her while she showed it off, being careful to pose the cheese so that the name ORKNEY could be seen right way up. When she left the shop, surrounded by the local press, she posed in brilliant sunlight and indicated where I was to be; the bright light made her squint and made me cringe. There she waited for the camera to respond. This kind of photography is anathema to me—the posed, predictable shot. At the moment there seemed nothing to do but to go along with her setups.

I sought out Gordon Reece, her P.R. adviser, to explain how I worked and what I was trying to achieve; that the idea was to follow her through her day's activities, to see her in

1977
Mrs. Thatcher in the Orkneys with an Orkney cheese.

action in relationship to other people, to get her away from her desk, but at work and at ease; that the picture profile must be done without posing, otherwise the spontaneity and the personality would not come through. Implicit in this was the idea that she would shortly be going to the polls, and the voters would want a personal look at their candidate.

I had thought about talking to her myself but feared that it might tip her over into self-consciousness. Besides which, this was what she was like, this too was a facet of her character, and so part of the assignment. Also, I was curious to see where she would lead us, because I had never seen such naked will except in newborn infants, whose whole implacable mechanism for survival works overtime, demanding of life what is their due. Whether Gordon Reece spoke to her or not did not seem to matter; she did not stop directing me, and I, perhaps foolishly, went along, frustrated but intrigued.

Feeling totally dissatisfied with myself and my Thatcher pictures, and praying that Mrs. Gandhi would be easier to portray, I took off for India to join Bruce Chatwin. Mrs. Gandhi could not have been in greater contrast: an experienced politician, knowing and wily about the way of the press and the way of the world, tough and ruthless, clever and manipulative; she would turn on at will charm, anger, or whatever emotion was required.

I was to stay for two months, travelling with her, Bruce, and her entourage while she electioneered throughout Uttar Pradesh for a Muslim woman for Parliament, using this time to test her own chances for a comeback. We got along famously. She was knowledgeable about pictures and anxious for space in the British and world press. She quickly discovered that the story on her would be syndicated worldwide by my agency, Magnum Photos, and knowing that the space required for a picture story would yield more column inches than words would, she paid my camera a lot of attention. Some days she was attentive and kind to Chatwin when he interviewed her, some days she was curt with him, but with me she was always receptive and friendly.

One day, on a plane trip from Benares to Delhi, she asked me what my next assignment was. I smiled, thinking of my return to complete the story on the other prime minister hopeful, and of the difference between the two women. She asked me why I was smiling. Of course, I couldn't tell her, and simply said that the next job was to finish a cover story on Mrs. Thatcher. Mrs. Thatcher? She was irritated. It seemed lèse majesté.

Memories of this exchange were still with me when, on my return to London, Michael Rand called and asked to see the Thatcher pictures. It was time to tell the truth. The pictures were pretty static, and there was no story line. Michael pooh-poohed this — "Come on, don't put yourself down, I'm sure they're fine," and from me, "They're not right." We arranged for him to stop by that evening to check out the pictures. Over a glass of wine, he had to agree they were not right. What to do? I suggested that he get Snowdon to shoot her. Even with her reputation for not liking photographers she would be impressed with him. Also, she had picked up a reputation for not caring much for journalists and women, and Tony was neither. He could do her in a studio or in a situation where she would feel more at home, and she would certainly cooperate with him.

While we were talking, the phone rang. It was Gordon Reece, to ask if I would do the Conservative Party a favour. What? Do pictures of Mrs. Thatcher in the footsteps of Churchill. How do I do that? There was a sculptor friend of Churchill's, Oscar Nemon, who was currently doing a bust of Maggie and I could use the statues he had done of the great man as background. Would I do pictures on Saturday? I would indeed.

Saved! Chastened, I went the next day to Mr. Nemon's beautiful grace-and-favour studio. There stood vast uncast statues of Britain's saviour in the garden: a six-foot cube acting as a plinth on which there was a neck-less head of Churchill, a nine-foot striding figure, and numerous small maquettes, all realistic and in the heroic mould. I checked it all out, tried to calculate the light for the next day, had a talk with the sculptor, and on the way home promised myself that now it was to be my turn to call the shots.

When Margaret Thatcher arrived the following day, she was made up, complete with blue eyeshadow and newly pressed hair. A pretty woman, but one without the authority and style we see today. She wore an inexpensive blue-and-yellow dress (the party colours) of some man-made fibre. She pumped my hand. I admonished myself, silently, that it was my turn to direct—Mrs. Thatcher, will you stand here, and here, and here. Within fifteen minutes we had it all. The more insightful story on the agenda was replaced by the more or less set-up shots, against the background of her choice. The last round was still hers.

On the tenth anniversary of her tenure as Prime Minister (the longest of any P.M. in 150 years—and one of the most controversial), with the litany of love and the rhetoric of hate that surrounded her assailing us from the printed word and the electronic press, and the physical and sartorial changes that she and her packagers had wrought in her appearance and her persona—her voice was octaves lower and almost a purr, her hair beautifully coiffed, her clothes elegant, her teeth improved, she smiled more readily (Mitterrand is supposed to have instructed an aide who was to have dealings with her to watch her "Caligula-like eyes and her Marilyn Monroe lips")—it was hard to recognise the uncertain, anxiety-ridden woman whom I had photographed a decade before.

An image returned to me of the day in 1978 when Mrs. Gandhi spoke to me about her. We were on a plane from Benares to Delhi. Mrs. Gandhi was dressed in an elegant cotton sari (it was pre-monsoon, and cotton was more absorbent as well as more appropriate than silk for a tour seeking votes among the poor). She leaned back against the plane seat and said, "You know, when Mrs. Thatcher was here she was so tense I felt like telling her, 'If you're that nervous you'll never make Prime Minister.'"

1961
Lord Bath
with cronies
on his
Longleat
estate,
Wiltshire,
during a
Saturday
morning
shoot for
pheasant.

(LEFT)
1965
A meeting of
Brides of
Christ on
their
wedding day
to their Lord
at the
nunnery in
Godalming,
Surrey.

(RIGHT)
1961
One of four
girls who
share a flat
in Knights-
bridge.

1961
Remem-
brance
Sunday
Services at
Northleach,
Gloucester-
shire.

1965
Women's
Royal Army
Corps Band at
Liphook,
Hampshire.

1978
A protester at
a political
rally in
Southall, West
London.

1961
The Reverend
Leslie Ward,
Vicar of
Northleach,
Gloucester-
shire, at tea.

1964
John Bloom,
washing
machine
tycoon,
checking a
balance sheet
at home in
London's
West End.

1961
Mrs. Veronica Briggs, mathematics teacher, gives a tutorial at Wycombe Abbey, Buckinghamshire.

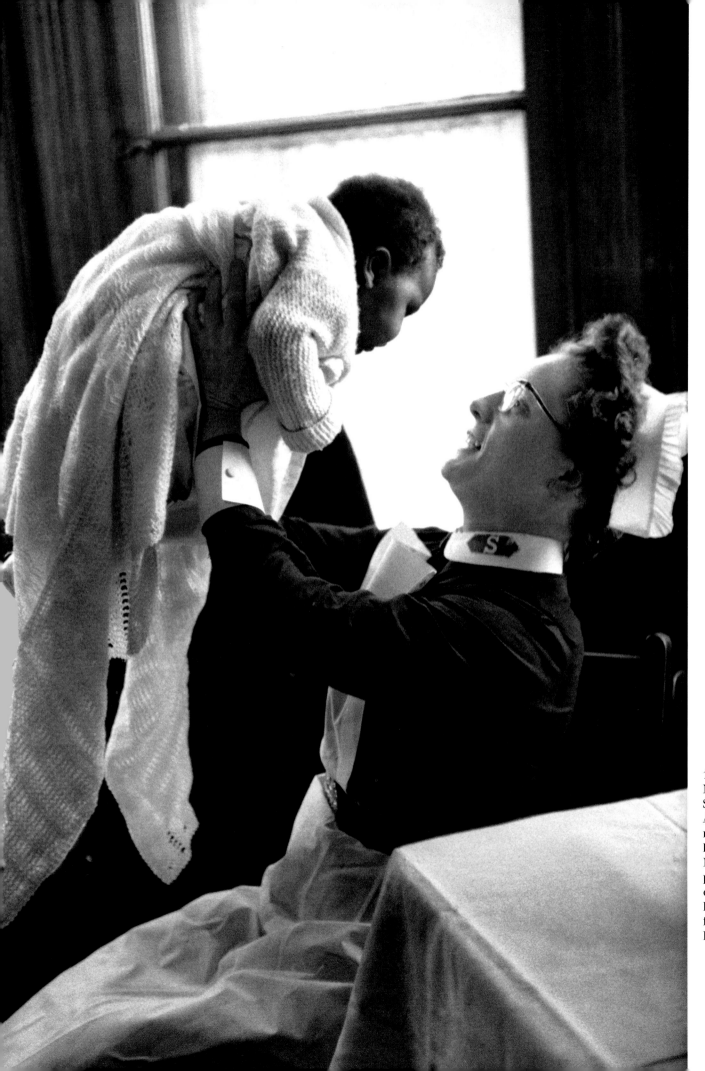

1962
Nurse in
Salvation
Army
maternity
home in
Manchester
plays with a
child before
his departure
for a foster
home.

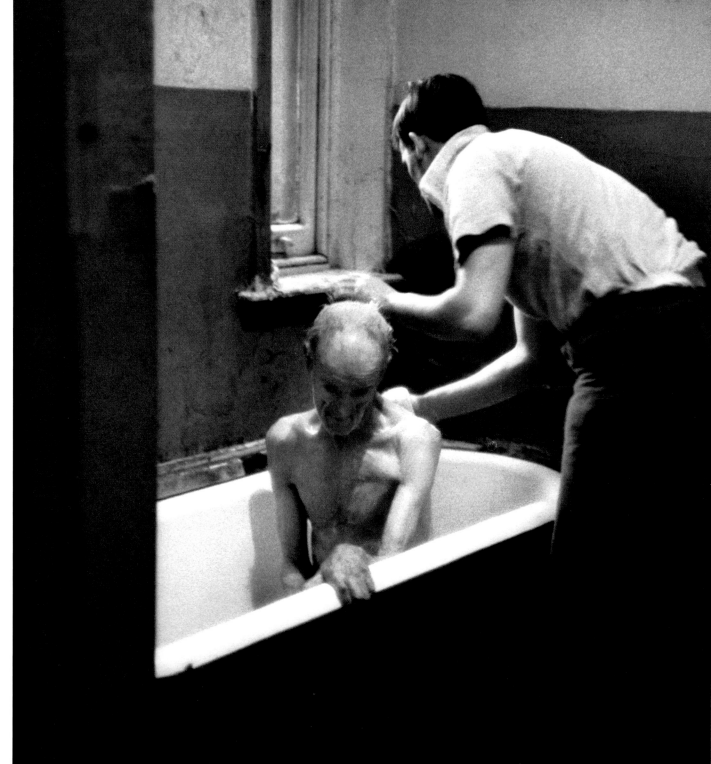

1962
A war injury made him unemploy-able, unable even to bathe himself. He found a home with the Salvation Army in Manchester.

1962
Salvation Army
prayers in
Manchester.

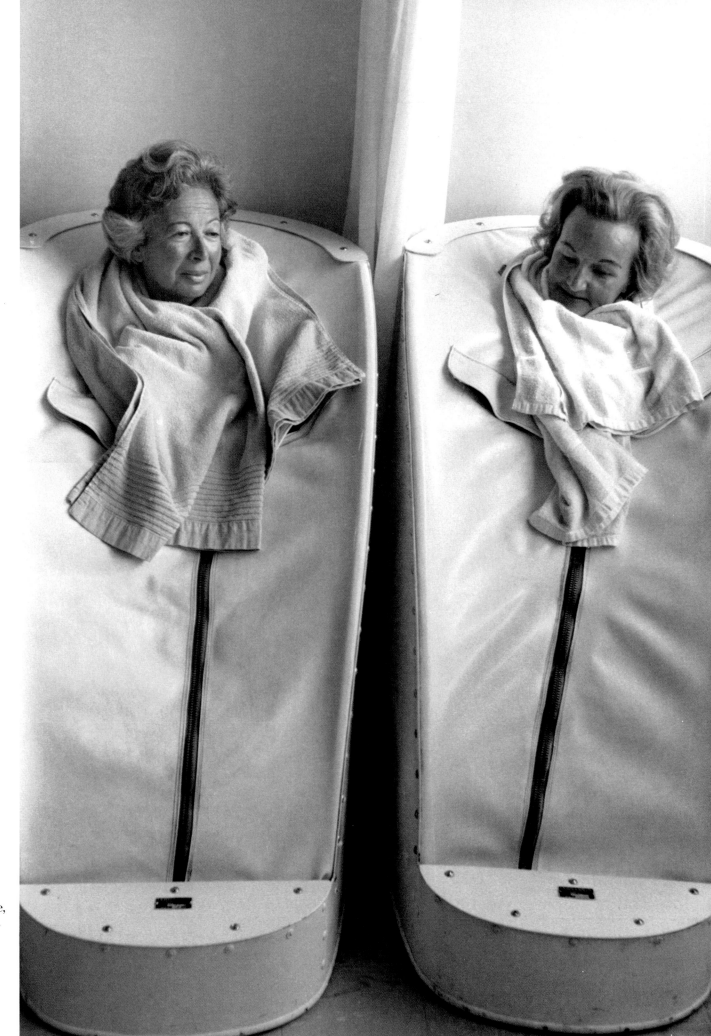

1965
Reducing
salon at
Forest Mere,
Hampshire.

1963
Reginald
Maudling,
Chancellor
of the
Exchequer,
on his
farm in
Hertfordshire
right before
Budget Day.

1963
Dr. Michael
Ramsey,
Archbishop of
Canterbury,
Primate of
the Church of
England, at
Canterbury
Cathedral,
Kent.

1963
Father
Gregory
Wilkins,
Director of
the Society of
the Sacred
Mission at
Kelham,
Nottingham-
shire.
Everyone
helps with
the chores.

(OVERLEAF)
1963
Contralto
Delia Woolford
auditions at
Morley
College,
London.

(LEFT)
1963
A pupil
practises at
Yehudi
Menuhin's
school in a
converted
hotel in
Kensington.

(RIGHT)
1963
Samuel
Spinak, free-
lance violinist
at the
Musicians'
Union Hall,
London.

1963
The living Richard
Burton poses for
an effigy of Becket
to be used in the
film of the same
name. Shepperton
Studios, Middlesex.

1963
Peter O'Toole being
borne in triumph (to a
party at the Dorchester
Hotel in London in his
honour on opening night
of *Hamlet*) in the arms of
his wife, Sîan Phillips.

1969
Extras in the film of *Anne of the Thousand Days* await the call to work. They rest on the lawn of Hever Castle, Kent, where Henry VIII met Anne Boleyn.

1963
Margot
Fonteyn and
Rudolf
Nureyev at a
dress
rehearsal for
*Marguerite
and Armand*
at the Royal
Opera House,
Covent
Garden,
London.

1964
Sir Alec
Douglas-
Home, the
Prime
Minister, and
Lady
Douglas-
Home at their
home, the
Hirsel, at
Lanark. The
Scottish
estate
comprises
sixty
thousand
acres.

(LEFT)
1964
A member of
the Royal
Toxophilite
Society
(founded in
1781), in
Bayswater,
London.

(RIGHT)
1964
A member of
the Royal
Society for
Protection
of Birds.
London.

1961
Midmorning
milk
"break" at
Cheltenham
Ladies'
College,
Gloucester-
shire.

1963
Sir Adrian
Boult
teaching a
student
musical
conducting at
the Royal
College of
Music,
London.

1963
A midsummer
journey from
the Inner
Hebrides to
Mull in
Scotland.

1965
A lesbian wedding in Clapham Common, South London. The groom is twenty years old and the bride fifty.

1963
John Huston,
the film
director, with
his dogs at St.
Clarens, his
home in
Ireland.

(LEFT)
1965
Edward
Heath, the
week after
being named
head of the
Conservative
Party, goes
for a swim on
the French
Riviera. The
underwater
photographer
is a *Life*
staffer.

(RIGHT)
1965
Edward
Heath—a
view of
himself as a
future Prime
Minister—at
home at
Albany,
Mayfair,
London.

1966
A butler
prepares the
silver for a
debutante's
ball in
London.

1977
A gunsmith
checks a
second-hand
gun intended
for sale in a
third world
country.
Manchester.

(LEFT)
1965
The Duke of Norfolk with his wife and four daughters and four of his dogs at Arundel Castle, West Sussex.

(RIGHT)
1966
Prince Philip, the Queen's Consort, prepares for a polo game at Windsor Great Park, Berkshire.

1966
A local
photographer
with his
props to
amuse his
children
clients.
Brighton
Beach, West
Sussex.

1966
Norman
Parklinson, the
photographer,
in London at
a *Vogue*
studio shoot
with Celia
Hammond,
one of the
famous
sixties
models.

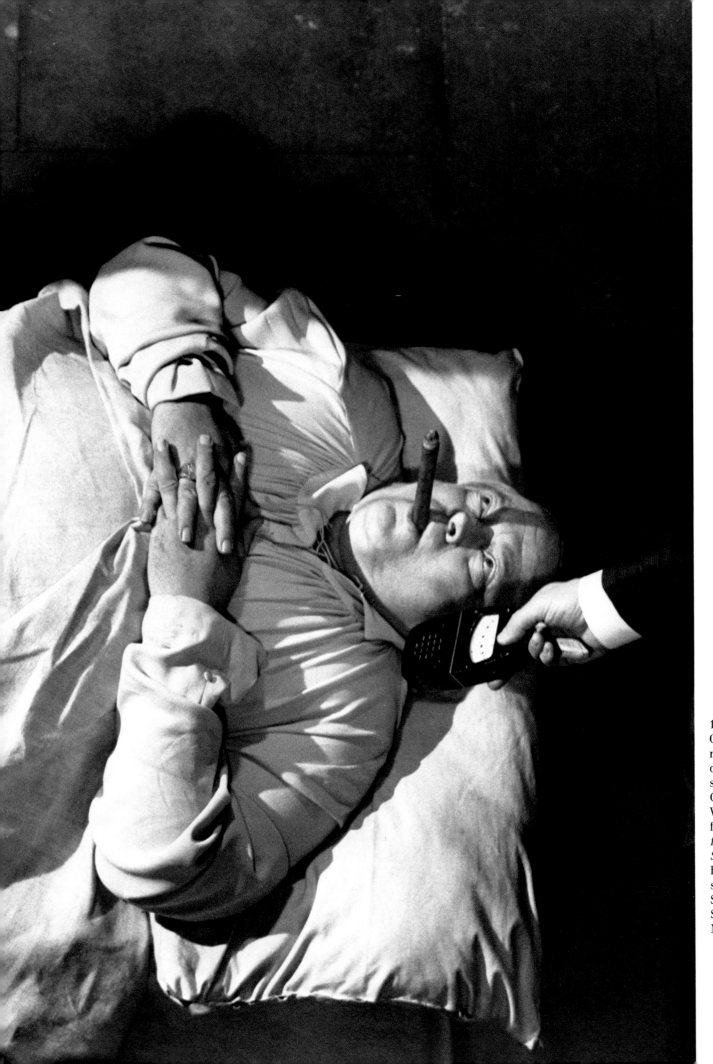

1966
Orson Welles rehearses the deathbed scene as Cardinal Wolsey in the film *A Man for All Seasons* on a British sound stage. Shepperton Studios, Middlesex.

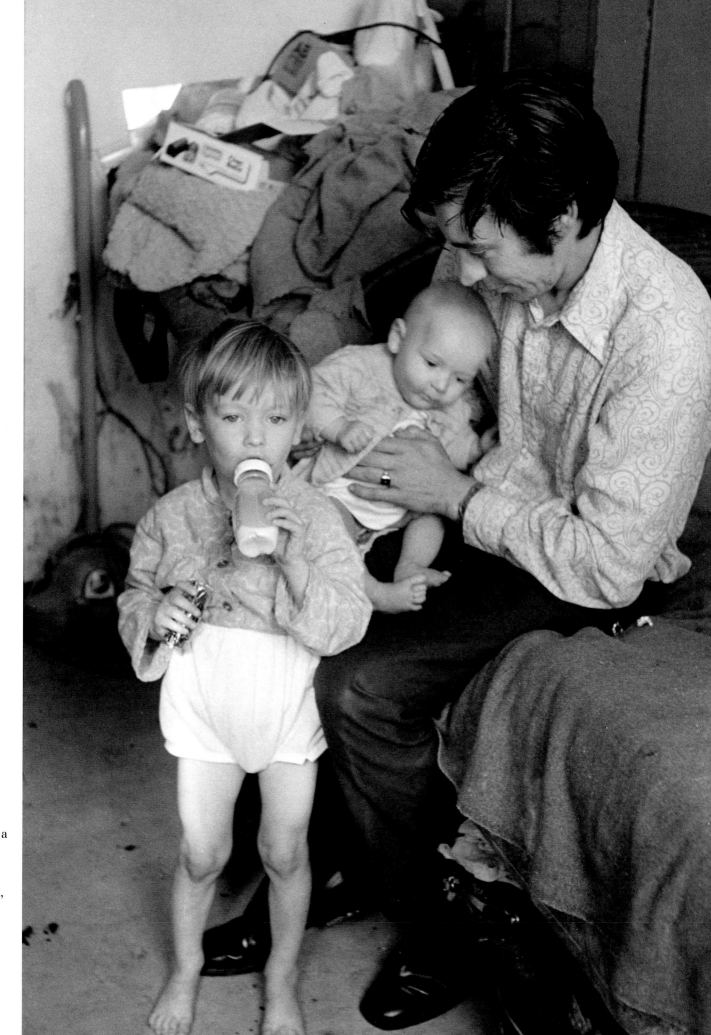

1972
Life within a
Greater
London
Council flat
in Lambeth,
South
London.

1967
Members of a
"therapeutic
community,"
where the
organisation
is run
democratically
by its
handicapped
member-
inmates.
The Borders.

1964
Her father is
the ruler of
an African
kingdom. She
is delivered
daily to the
French Lycée
by an English
chauffeur in
a Bentley.
Kensington,
West London.

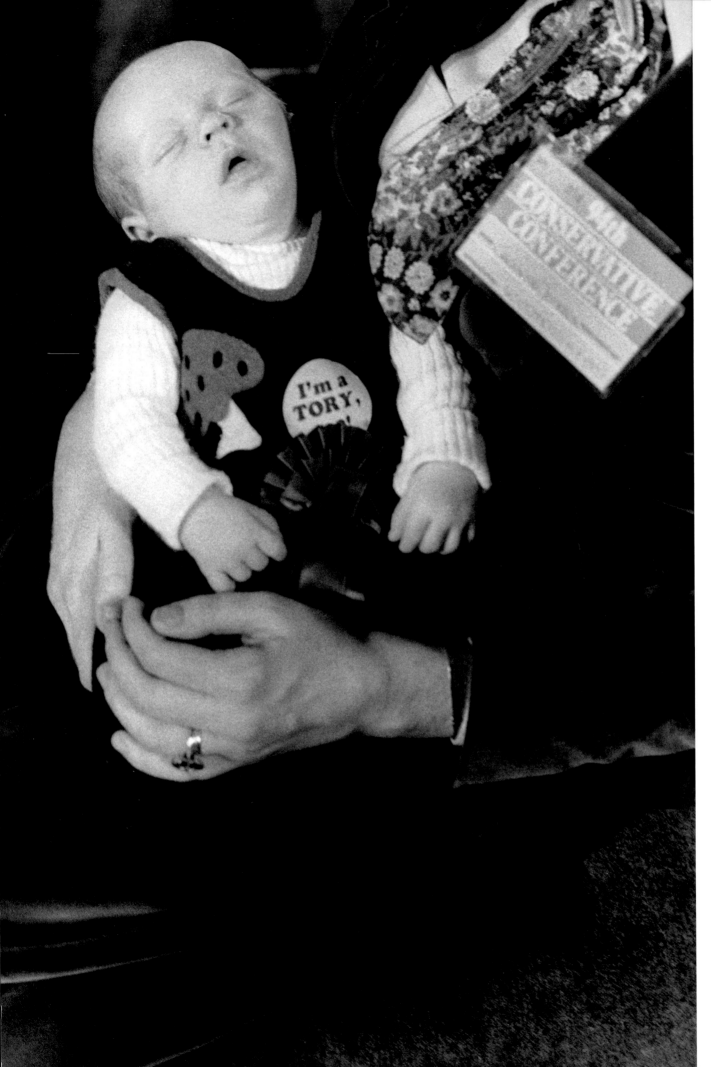

(LEFT)
1977
The
Conservative
Party
Conference in
Blackpool,
Lancashire.

(RIGHT)
1977
Margaret
Thatcher
electioneering
in the
Orkneys,
Scotland.

A Note on the Type

The text of this book was set in Walbaum, a type face designed by Justus Erich Walbaum in 1810. Walbaum was active as a type founder in Goslar and Weimar from 1799 to 1836. Though letterforms in this face are patterned closely on the "modern" cuts then being made by Giambattista Bodoni and the Didot family, they are of a far less rigid cut. Indeed, it is the slight but pleasing irregularities in the cut that give this face its human quality and account for its wide appeal. Even in appearance, Walbaum jumps boundaries, having a more French than German look.

Color Separations by Accent On Color,
Hauppauge, New York

Printed by Van Dyck Printing Company,
North Haven, Connecticut

Composed by The Sarabande Press, New York, New York

Bound by Horowitz/Rae Book Manufacturers,
Fairfield, New Jersey

Typography and binding design by Holly McNeely